17.05
2165
D0050445

THE CURRICULUM

Purpose, Substance, Practice

375.001
F749c

THE CURRICULUM

Purpose, Substance, Practice

ARTHUR WELLESLEY FOSHAY

Foreword by O. L. Davis, Jr.

Teachers College, Columbia University
New York and London

81141

Christian Heritage
College Library
2100 Greenfield Dr.
El Cajon, CA 92019

Published by Teachers College Press, 1234 Amsterdam Avenue, New York, NY 10027

Copyright © 2000 by Teachers College, Columbia University

All rights reserved. No part of this publication may be reproduced or transmitted in any form or by any means, electronic or mechanical, including photocopy, or any information storage and retrieval system, without permission from the publisher.

Lines from "Physiologus" and "After This, Sea," by Josephine Miles, from *Collected Poems 1930–83*. Copyright 1983 by Josephine Miles. Used with the permission of the Poet and the University of Illinois Press.

Library of Congress Cataloging-in-Publication Data

Foshay, Arthur Wellesley, 1912–
  The curriculum : purpose, substance, practice / Arthur Wellesley Foshay.
    p. cm.
  Includes bibliographical references (p.) and index.
  ISBN 0-8077-3936-7 — ISBN 0-8077-3935-9 (pbk.)
  1. Curriculum planning—United States. 2. Education—Curricula—
Philosophy. I. Title.

  LB2806.15 .F66 2000
  375'.001'0973—dc21

                                     99-053667

ISBN 0-8077-3935-9 (paper)
ISBN 0-8077-3936-7 (cloth)

Printed on acid-free paper

Manufactured in the United States of America

07 06 05 04 03 02 01 00   8 7 6 5 4 3 2 1

This book is dedicated to the memory of Hollis L. Caswell,
mentor, advisor, colleague, coauthor, and friend.

Contents

Foreword

Years into his official retirement, Arthur W. Foshay systematically began to theorize about curriculum. He was well prepared for this work. Certainly, he brought to the task a rich liberal and professional education. He possessed abundant practical experience as teacher and principal and, later, as researcher, consultant, and productive scholar. He understood the work of many of his predecessors and colleagues, not just those in education, but individuals whose scholarship featured inquiries in fields as disparate as psychology, poetry, sociology, and music. Moreover, his curriculum theorizing developed strikingly differently than had others. He named his formulation The Curriculum Matrix and, in its three-dimensional depiction, he emphasized basic dimensions of curriculum considerations and their interactions. With the matrix, he sought to symbolize the immense complexity of curriculum decisions even as he elevated explicit attention to specific matters. Foshay, to be sure, wrote about the matrix as a theory. I believe, however, that he did not see it only as an elaborated body of theoretic prescriptions. Rather, I sense that he recognized the matrix as a type of reasoned checklist of considerations for use by practitioners as they dealt with curriculum problems.

I first encountered Foshay's matrix more than a decade ago; he had mailed me a working draft manuscript and requested my reactions. The manuscript featured an abbreviated description of the matrix and an explication of the relationship of what he then called "spirituality" and mathematics. I confess to having become instantly engaged by his arguments. My experience was not transcendent, as I recall, but it was intense. I immediately was aware that I could never again think about curriculum without considering his fresh conception. In retrospect, I believe that my judgement was accurate. I have pursued curriculum meanings with the matrix and I have used successive drafts of that first paper in my teaching.

Although I never took courses with Professor Foshay, he was my teacher for almost 40 years. We met when he became President-elect of the Association for Supervision and Curriculum Development and I was a member of the ASCD staff. As our friendship grew, he became "Wells" rather than "Dr. Foshay." More substantively, both the breadth and depth of his scholarship and experience increasingly impressed me. When he talked as a group member, all of us listened and learned. He also learned from us—and told us so. His 1961 ASCD presidential address[1] broke new intellectual ground for a few of us as much as it near-offended some of his longtime associates. Unlike some of his colleagues, Wells continued to learn and to develop new and carefully reasoned positions. For years, he and I enjoyed at least one evening of dinner and conversation when we met at the ASCD annual conference and at other meetings.

After I read his first paper about the matrix, Wells and I increased our interactions. We almost always talked about his current work on the matrix or some of its elements and his meanings. I also encouraged him to publish his papers. He conscientiously delayed the submission of his first major manuscript about the matrix, however, until he was confident that he had written it as precisely and gracefully as he could.

Preparation of that essay, of course, was a daunting project. In it, Wells treated the intersection of mathematics and spirituality. He confessed that he knew less about both of these fields than he knew about some other elements and interactions in the matrix. Also, he considered that his illumination of this superficially unlikely interaction might encourage the explication of other interactions, and thus extend the possible meanings within the idea of the matrix. In the process, he changed "spirituality" to "transcendence"—a difficult decision, but one that likely reduced the possibility of easy, knee-jerk rejections of his ideas.[2]

Over the next 7 years, Wells wrote and published manuscripts that focused on the intersections of each of his other five purposes with a particular school subject. He submitted these papers to the *Journal of Curriculum and Supervision*. Each underwent peer review and none escaped suggested revisions and sharp critical remarks. As editor of the journal, I commonly wrote him extended remarks about each new manuscript. Always with mindful grace, he expressed thanks to all reviewers; he usually revised some aspects of his manuscripts on the basis of the reviews, but, on some matters, he did not budge. Wells sincerely wished that other curriculum scholars would engage him in conversation about his ideas and I believe that he was disappointed when many of his friends and readers did not. He frequently remarked that he developed the matrix for several personal reasons: He believed that it meaningfully related essential curriculum concerns; he understood further that his matrix constituted his personal and grateful response to the curriculum field for its generosity to him throughout his career and retirement years; and he also believed that his responsibility to the field included his obligation to continue to contribute to it rather than only to take from it.

This book contains all of Wells' essays about the curriculum matrix. He completed the book before his death in April of 1998, and its publication by Teachers College Press marks, in a special way, his return to the College that he loved. The book does not include reactions or expansions or critiques of his positions. They will come in the future. In effect, this book is both landmark and invitation.

Wells recognized that his work on the matrix was neither comprehensive nor complete. For example, at an AERA session in San Diego, he commented in his final public statement that he wanted to direct his attention to social context more than he previously had done. Regrettably, he never had the time to write another paper. This book exists as an invitation to others to do what he could not continue and what only they can do. I am confident that Wells would hope that, among their responses, they would think beyond his beginnings.

In the future, I want to encourage, sponsor, and, possibly, undertake several inquiries within the spirit of Wells' matrix. For example, Wells formulated his set of purposes from his conviction that the school curriculum should contribute to a person's becoming a fully human individual. These purposes, within the noble aspirations of liberal education, focus on curriculum for individuals. Still, I have wondered about the role of other reasonable and problematic but excluded purposes. I do not believe, for instance, that his "social" purpose sufficiently encompasses the long-standing American emphasis of a "civic" purpose of schooling. Furthermore, the publicly articulated economic purpose of human capital formation properly cannot be ignored as a purpose. Continued concern about curriculum purposes simply must not be marginalized. Very importantly, also, explication of his dimensions of "practice," only recently initiated, should accelerate.[3] Adequate responses, as well, must be fashioned to rebut critiques that insist that the matrix is flawed by "linearity" and the "hard edges" of its categories, attributes that Foshay certainly never embraced. He never privileged, in his matrix, any purpose or any dimension of practice; he understood that, in practical curriculum endeavors, people who work toward decisions will pursue their endeavors differently and from different starting points. Another important consideration surely will focus on the nature and use of evidence employed by individuals within groups who seek decisions to curriculum problems. Wells, I believe, would like this idea; he was an early leader of "action research" as efforts to inform curriculum decisions.[4] Surely needed, also, is attention to the nature of community within which curriculum decisions are deliberated, made, and engaged in practice. These few ideas do not constitute an agenda. Rather, they are some of the matters that have sprung from my efforts to think with and to foster my students' thinking about the matrix. They deserve serious attention in our continuing pursuit of meanings.

I welcome scholars and students to Foshay's curriculum matrix. I hope that those who already have read his essays discover fresh ideas in their revisit. For those who come to this book without prior awareness of or engagement with the matrix, I trust that they will employ a panoply of formulations and concerns to launch their own consideration of his substantive ideas and of their possible roles in curriculum practice. Our participation in these activities will honor both Wells Foshay's and our own common commitment to curriculum inquiry.

O. L. Davis, Jr.
Professor of Curriculum and Instruction
The University of Texas at Austin

NOTES

1. Arthur W. Foshay, "A Modest Proposal," *Educational Leadership* 18 (May 1961): 506–516.

2. Arthur W. Foshay, "The Curriculum Matrix: Transcendence and the Curriculum," *Journal of Curriculum and Supervision* 6 (Summer 1991): 277–293.

3. Jennifer Deets, "Russian Language in Schools: A Conceptual Critique of the Foshay Curriculum Matrix" (doctoral dissertation, The University of Texas at Austin, 1998); also, Jennifer Deets, "Curriculum Costs," *The Curriculum Journal* 9(Summer 1998): 211–225.

4. See, for example, Arthur W. Foshay and Kenneth D. Wann, *Children's Social Values, an Action Research Study* (New York, Bureau of Publications, Teachers College, Columbia University 1951); Arthur W. Foshay and James A. Hall (Eds.), *Research for Curriculum Improvement*, 1957 Yearbook of the Association for Supervision and Curriculum Development (Washington, DC: Association for Supervision and Curriculum Development, 1957); Arthur W. Foshay, "Action Research: An Early History in the United States," *Journal of Curriculum and Supervision* 9(Summer, 1994): 317–325.

Acknowledgments

I wish to express my gratitude to Angela Fraley Foshay, who has helped at every stage in the development of this book in both small and large ways. My son, Wellesley R. Foshay, was particularly helpful in the development of Chapter 7. O. L. Davis, Jr. provided sustained encouragement throughout the development of the work. Others who have offered advice and specific suggestions are Kay Alexander, a nationally known consultant on Art Education, formerly of the Palo Alto school district; James Carse of New York University; and the late George Riggan, formerly of the Hartford Theological Seminary. In addition, I am deeply indebted to colleagues, too many to name, whose willingness to discuss and debate issues has brought true gratification to my life and work over the years.

Introduction

The curriculum is best thought of as a plan for action by students and teachers. Like any plan, its goals, its substance, and the details of the action it requires must be clear. Here, we shall examine these three dimensions of the curriculum. We will organize it around its *purposes*, or goals, the *substance* of the school curriculum, which has been determined by tradition and the necessities required for participation in our Western culture, and the action, or *practice*, which consists of the behavior of students as directed/encouraged by teachers.

As a field of study and experimentation, the curriculum has always suffered from lack of specificity and from the casual influence of political and cultural events and pressures. There is broad agreement that the curriculum should serve the needs of society—whatever that is taken to mean—and that schooling should help students to maximize their potentialities—whatever that is taken to mean. It is the precise meaning of these terms that has remained unspecified. In consequence, the curriculum as a field of theory and research has been in disarray and subject to special pleading ever since its emergence early in the twentieth century.

Many of these special pleas have had merit. Nobody objects, for example, to the idea that the American public school should prepare students for citizenship in our democracy. Similarly, it is obvious that teachers should fit the curriculum to the developmental needs of growing young people. Of course, students should read the Great Books, and they should be prepared vocationally, as well. Social problems such as racial and gender injustice should be addressed. Schools should develop basic skills. Costs should be examined closely, and so on. Every one of these suggestions has merit and ought to be addressed.

However, observation of classrooms in actual schools makes it evident that, although some teachers deal with some of these matters, by and large, classrooms have not changed. One reason for this stasis is that the special pleas are incomplete. A goal is stated broadly but left unspecified, and its substance and practice are left to be inferred. Or a practice is advocated, but no goal is stated. Thus, in many cases worthy ideas are distorted and disappear, and changes are random and temporary.

That is why school reform during the twentieth century has generally failed. Who remembers the Gary Plan? What has become of the Project Method? Why are Montessori schools rare and private? What is really basic? These once promising reforms, and many others, became buzz words, were distorted in application, and have largely disappeared.

A popular current assessment of the problem is that the public schools have no competition and therefore do not change. That belief has led to several proposals for reorganization of the schools, such as charter schools, educational vouchers, and home schooling. In other words, take schooling out of the hands of those now in charge and give it to others. But changing the administration or the form of the school does not necessarily mean the substance of the school experience—the school curriculum—will change. It is as if, to improve medical practice, one added a floor to a hospital. As this is written, it is being proposed that national standards be established through the imposition of uniform examinations. Because this would have the effect of producing a nationally standardized offering (teachers always teach to the tests), it, too, is likely to fail. We need a better way of thinking about school improvement.

There was a time when Science seemed to offer such a way. Educational leaders attempted to form a Science of Education. While some of the attributes of Science were imported into Education, such as objective measurement, no Science of Education has emerged.

The problem underlying all of this is vagueness of purpose. Ernest Nagel and Thomas Kuhn suggest a solution to the problem. Nagel (1968, p. 7) says, "It is undoubtedly the case that the sciences are organized bodies of knowledge and that in all of them a classification of their materials into significant types or kinds . . . is an indispensable task." Kuhn (1970) points out that organized fields of knowledge rest on paradigms, the parts of which are specified.

Various organizations of the curriculum field have been offered. Based on the idea that the school curriculum consists of school experiences, forces that shape experience have been named—stage of growth, societal context, cultural traditions, and others. These have been rendered as charts, Venn diagrams, concentric circles, and other figures.

What continues to be lacking is a clear-cut statement of a curriculum organization that would specify the *purposes* to be served by schooling; the *substance* of school experience that arises from the purposes, yet is influenced by cultural tradition, societal needs, and the needs of growing young people; and school *practice*, which brings the purposes and the substance to reality.

In what follows, the general purpose of schooling is taken to be the development of a sense of self that includes the principal attributes of humanness. Stated differently, the general purpose of education is to bring to reality those things that make us human. This has been called "the development of individual potentialities" or "self-actualization" (Maslow, 1971, p. 162). It is important to recognize that these statements of purpose include, but go far beyond, what are often given as the purposes of schooling—to prepare for a job, to become an effective citizen in our democracy, and to get into college.

While each of these is a worthy purpose, none of them is complete. Getting high grades in school, although obviously desirable, misrepresents the purposes of education, as is shown by the low correlation between school grades and success in life (no matter how it is measured). The correlation, once mentioned to me by Benjamin Bloom (in conversation), is around .3, which amounts to only 9% of the variance.

As we explore the substance of the curriculum—the usual school subjects—we shall see that they acquire depth when they serve the stated purposes of effective humanness. Our examination of these possibilities will be far from complete, because every part of the curriculum is itself enormously complex and because all the parts interact, as is explained in the discussion of the Curriculum Matrix in Chapter 1.

Although hints at how all of this is to be done in classroom practice are presented, no attempt has been made to offer a complete plan of action. Such a plan would consume many volumes, given the complexity of the curriculum field. Experienced teachers, however, may find in these pages suggestions and openings that they can use as they fashion classroom offerings.

Here, we shall see what the curriculum would be if the grand, all-inclusive purpose of formal education were taken to be to help children grow into full realization of themselves as human beings. Preparing for an occupation is part of this larger purpose; getting along with other people is part of it; becoming a good citizen is part of it; becoming a responsible parent is part of it; gaining a grasp of the academic skills is part of it. Each of these parts is essential, but all of them together are not the whole of it. The whole of it is to become the realized self—to bring to reality as much of one's potentiality as possible. That is what the approach to the school curriculum described here seeks to bring about.

CHAPTER 1

The Curriculum Matrix

The curriculum is often defined as the summation and meaning of one's experience. From this viewpoint, there is the school curriculum, which concerns us here, and the life curriculum, which includes all of one's experiences.

To view the school curriculum as the summation of school experience is at once to recognize its complexity. Because experience is an individual affair, each person's school curriculum is unique. Because one's school curriculum includes *all* school experience, there is no logical way to put boundaries around it. Because the life curriculum deals with one's entire life, it, too, is boundless. The curriculum is as boundless as the universe of experience. How, then, shall it be organized? How shall one study it or experiment with it?

One way the curriculum has been organized renders the field as a model, thus providing an orderly way to examine it. Given its boundless complexity, however, the most appropriate model for the curriculum would be the universe itself, with all the parts interacting; but no such model could be constructed.

This complexity and boundlessness explains why the existing models of the curriculum are unsatisfactory. One model represents the curriculum as an array of concentric circles, with the individual at the center. Another represents it as a Venn diagram, with the various spheres intersecting. Yet another shows it as a chart, with something apparently axiomatic at the top and a series of experiences descending from it. None of these models has suggested the specifics of purpose, substance, and practice.

Despite these difficulties, I shall represent the curriculum as a three-dimensional matrix, with the parts specified, in which it is assumed that all the parts interact. The matrix has the disadvantages of suggesting boundaries and predetermined sequences of interactions for this boundless, endlessly and complexly interacting field. It has the advantages, however, of offering specific components—of being specific—and of suggesting relationships that are often overlooked. If, in using this model, we will remember that it implies boundaries to something that is boundless, and simplicity where the actuality is highly complex, perhaps it can lead to action.

THE CURRICULUM MATRIX MODEL

The three dimensions of the Curriculum Matrix are its *purposes*, its *substance*, and the *practice* to be undertaken. Each of these dimensions consists of a number of specifics, which are shown in Figure 1.1.

The matrix is a model, or an organization, not a doctrine. The purposes of education might be different from those given here; so might the substance. The practices, however, remain the same, regardless of changes in purpose or substance. For example, in a dictatorship, the broad purpose of education might be to make people obedient to the central government and to make them respect and obey the dictator. In an economy different from that in the United States, the whole purpose of education might be to train a work force. In an elite private school, the purpose might be to indicate how one should behave as a member of the upper class. The substance chosen would reflect these purposes and would be different from that given here. The school culture would also be different.

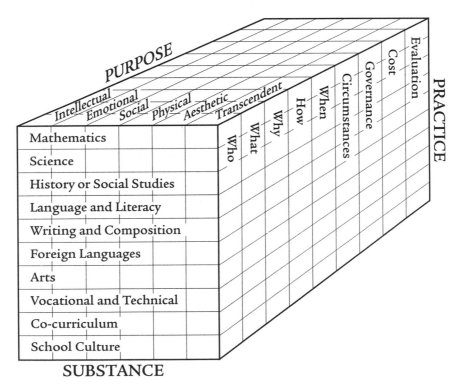

FIGURE 1.1. The Curriculum Matrix

In the matrix as given, the general purpose of education—to bring one's humanness to reality—is specified as including six subpurposes. There are ten substances and nine practices. Each of these specifics is itself complex, and each part interacts with all the others. There would be a theoretical $(6 \times 10 \times 9)^2 / 2 = 145{,}800$ interactions. Some of these would be bizarre and would be ignored. But most of the interactions actually take place as one teaches.

In this chapter, we shall review briefly the specifications for each of the three principal dimensions of the Curriculum Matrix. In subsequent chapters, each of the six purposes will be described and will be applied in depth to an unlikely school subject; there will also be brief illustrations of how it may appear in the other principal school subjects. We will examine these purposes in the reverse order of their familiarity: first the transcendent, then the aesthetic, the physical, the social, the emotional, and the intellectual.

THE PURPOSE

The general *purpose* of education is to bring a full sense of one's self to awareness or realization. This general purpose has been analyzed into six aspects, which become subordinate curriculum purposes.

The Transcendent Self

The transcendent experience is generally overlooked in teaching. What is it? What it is *not* is a specifically religious experience; that is, it does not inherently deal with, or arise from, any particular religious belief or dogma. The experience is described both by psychologists and theologians.

Psychologically, the experience is a sudden awareness of one's self as a part of a vastly larger whole. The experience is dramatic, and it goes beyond logic. When students have this experience in school, it arises from a sudden recognition of the vast context within which a particular understanding (often, in a subject field) arises. It is, of course, unusual, even rare, in school. It is a private experience; a teacher cannot know that it has happened unless a student speaks of it. But it happens. In mathematics, as we shall see, it is a sudden identification of one's self with a great imaginative event in math history, such as when some prehistoric person said "Let this pebble stand for a horse." That person, for the first time ever, used a symbol to make an abstraction. No other animal had ever done that. To be able to abstract is to be distinctively human. To abstract is to find a bit of one's own humanity—to join the human race.

The experience of transcendence is a universal part of human development. We all wonder at our own existence; all of us wonder who we are. Some of us suddenly realize ourselves as a part of a vastly larger whole.

The transcendent experience must be distinguished from the more familiar "aha!" experience. The transcendent experience is a sudden enlargement of the self. The "aha!" experience is a sense of things suddenly falling into place, or into an organized whole.

Theologians have given one account after another of such sudden transcendent experiences, from ancient times to the present. We can consider the experience itself as they have described it, without entering into their specifically religious explanations of its meaning.

Although awareness of the transcendent experience is uncommon, the experience is nevertheless universal among human beings. Everyone knows, one way or another, that he or she is a precious, unique person. If this view of self were wholly lacking, the person would be less than human, and indeed would tend toward self-destruction.

The Aesthetic Self

Direct attention to the aesthetic experience is almost as rare in schools as attention to the transcendent. Like the transcendent experience, the aesthetic experience is extralogical. It is a realization that the form, content, and style of something fit one another exceptionally well, or do not. It involves aesthetic judgment—something is more or less beautiful or ugly. The aesthetic experience and the judgments that often accompany it are universal among us, like the other components of the self discussed in this book. Almost everything we sense has aesthetic value, be it intense or mild. Our dress, our speech, our ways of relating to others, the objects we deal with—all are more or less beautiful or ugly, these being the terms of aesthetic judgment. It is the universality of the aesthetic experience that is ignored in school, where, if it is attended to at all, it is consigned to the arts, which are too often viewed as mere entertainment. We shall see here that it is always present in all school activities and school subjects and that, deliberately or not, we always respond to the aesthetic qualities inherent in school activities as well as in our other activities and awarenesses.

The Physical Self

Like the transcendent and the aesthetic self, the physical self is not usually dealt with in school. Teachers are instructed to view the physical nature of the human being in terms of physical disorders and how they may be avoided, or in terms of athletics, or in the somewhat medieval sense that the body is inherently evil. Like our medieval ancestors, we want children to avoid "carnal knowledge." Adolescents learn to view their bodies as separate objects, not as a part of their complex selves.

Since 1950, teacher-training institutions have taken a broader view of the physical self. They have changed the names of their departments to "kinesiology," or "movement sciences," or to some other name that reflects a shift in emphasis from sports to more fundamental matters.

What are these more fundamental matters? They are suggested by some terms now common: *body language, physical expressiveness*, the *mind-body linkage*, and the like. Recognizing, as did those in medieval times, that there is nothing in the mind that is not first in the senses—that people are in a constant transaction with their environment—recent scholars in this field have studied this relationship and developed curriculum activities that the relationship implies. We shall examine the physical self in Chapter 4.

It is interesting that the separation of mind from body, along with the subordination of the body, is a specifically Western tradition. It has never existed in the Orient, where the various contemplative doctrines recognize the unity of all aspects of human existence.

The Social Self

The second three of the attributes of the self to be considered here—the social, the emotional, and the intellectual—have received far more attention by educators than have the three mentioned earlier. Of these last three, the social development of children has been the object of considerable curriculum attention during the present century.

The social aspect of the self is, of course, as essential to normal selfhood as is any one of the others. Like the other aspects of the self, if it were wholly missing from one's behavioral repertoire, one would be considered psychotic.

Until approximately 1900, teachers kept order in classes through what was thought of as disciplinary measures, which sometimes included corporal punishment. Social development, or the ability to function with other people, was left to the children.

With the beginnings of Progressive Education during the first decade of the present century, the development of the skills and attitudes necessary for successful participation in society was brought to awareness in the classroom for the first time. The classroom climate changed fundamentally. Children were encouraged to cooperate in small groups and to work on matters of social importance. There was some attention given to their moral development, where *moral* was taken to mean following social rules and ultimately developing a conscience. It came to be considered important that students enjoy school and that they look forward to school attendance.

The Progressive Education movement, which lasted from the first decade until the demise of the Progressive Education Association in 1957, stressed social development at the expense of the academic side of schooling. Development in the teaching of the academic subjects was left to the subject-matter organizations, and found its way into classrooms chiefly through texts and standardized tests. The Progressive Education emphasis on social development, and the accompanying practices, remain in schools today.

Social (including moral) development has been studied extensively during this century. While much remains to be discovered, this aspect of the self is now receiving attention for the first time in educational history.

The Emotional Self

All of us are emotional. Our attitude toward this fact, however, is conflicted. We seek pleasure, joy, and satisfaction, and we seek to avoid fear, shame, and guilt. As individuals, we seek what are called the positive emotions, and we seek to avoid the negative emotions.

But as teachers, we continue to act as if we lived in the eighteenth century. Samuel Johnson, in his eighteenth-century dictionary, defined passion as a "disturbance of the reason." In the study of emotion, we continue to seek ways to avoid negative emotions, such as anger and fear. We tend to ignore the positive emotions. We imply that, because emotions "disturb the reason," they should be avoided; we imply that a healthy individual is completely rational, which is to say a completely cold person. We speak of emotionality as if it were somehow abnormal and to be avoided like any other disorder.

It has become apparent in modern times that this old stereotypical view is mistaken. Ever since the emergence of psychiatry as a science, and therapy as a practice, it has been obvious that the emotions are a normal part of the self and that one of the purposes of schooling has to be to promote emotional development.

Like the other aspects of the self, the emotional self is complex. Because we can deal with only a small part of it here, we shall take the psychiatrist's view of the emotions. In therapy, psychiatrists seek to make their clients aware of their own emotions, so that they might discover the roots of their emotions in order to control those that are destructive and to exploit those that are constructive. In school, we can borrow the idea of awareness and can take as our purpose making students aware of the emotions. With such awareness comes emotional maturity.

We are teachers, however, not therapists, and the great majority of our students are emotionally healthy. What, then, can we do? We can deal with one aspect of awareness, namely, vocabulary. In the degree that people can give names to their feelings, they are aware of them in at least some degree. The development of such awareness can be taken as part of the purpose of education.

That is the position taken here. We shall examine the presence of emotion in history and other school subjects, intending to disclose both its universal and its inevitable quality, and also to make emotion available for discussion and thought in school by developing a vocabulary of emotion.

The Intellectual Self

Traditionally, the sole purpose of schooling has been the development of the intellect. Certainly, more is known about intellectuality in school than about any of the other components of the self we have discussed here. The research literature on intellectual development is rich and diverse. But it is surprising to find that there is no dominant theory of children's intellectual growth as there is, for example, concerning moral growth. Rather, there are many disparate studies of the various components of intellectuality, such as memory, reasoning, creativity, and imaginativeness. Likewise, associated with intellectual growth, motivation has come to be a popular object of attention. As a field of inquiry, intellectual development is a scattered, incompletely understood field.

Here, since the field is so complex, we shall attend to one prominent part—many would say, the central part—of intellectuality, that is, problem solving. There are several patterns recommended; Kagan's (1984, pp. 230–233) "executive processes" is one. These approaches have some things in common. Chief among them is this: to solve a problem, one must first somehow know what the solution would be like. One must somehow "see" the goal or the purpose. Without this, problems can only be explored, not solved. We have borrowed freely from the sources and have proposed a series of steps, or questions, that depend less on the context of a problem than do some of the other approaches.

We have applied this approach, first, to the arts, where one does not expect to find intellectuality, and more briefly to the other principal school subjects.

THE SUBSTANCE

We now turn to the second major dimension of the Curriculum Matrix, the *substance* of the offering. In educational jargon, what we call "substance" here is usually called "content." Substance seems to be a more accurate term, inasmuch as we deal here with school experience, some of which is unstructured.

The principal shortcoming of most teaching of organized substance is that it fails to examine the depths of its field. Dates, names, and events are taken to be History; map-reading substitutes for Geography; memorized paradigms are taken to be Mathematics; spelling and grammar take the place of writing, and so on. In general, instruction stops with skill, or know-how. Understanding, or "know-why," is not sought. The point of view taken here is that the academic school subjects are the names of the ways humankind has found to penetrate reality. It is these modes of behavior that students ought to learn. Each of the principal school subjects has its own symbol system—maps, numbers, special language or jargon, names of categories, systems of notation, and so on. These technical matters must, of course, become part of a student's knowledge. But if knowledge stops with factual material and skills—if that is all that appears on school tests— the student's understanding of the field in question is so superficial that it is usually called "merely academic," and high grades in school subjects have only a little to do with successful living.

Here, an attempt is made to go beyond technique to the modes of inquiry represented by each of the principal academic school subjects. History is taken to be, not a study of the past, for the past is gone, but an interpretation of what remains from the past in the present, the record. Mathematics is taken to be a series of astonishing leaps of human imagination, each of which is studied in school, perhaps through reinvention by students. Good literature is taken to be a venture into a world created by the author; it is much more than plot and character. Geography is taken to be a study of the ways human beings deal with the Earth's surface. It is much more than map reading and the naming of locations. And so on with the other school subjects. Each one is understood as a way to penetrate reality, and the student is expected to learn to employ these various ways.

As was pointed out earlier, what is taught in school—the experiences that are offered—is a function of the culture out of which the school itself emerges. Different cultures offer different patterns of experience. It follows that the school substance differs from one culture to another. The curriculum reflects the local governmental structure, local tastes and customs, and local preferences, and these differ in the various world cultures and social structures. Therefore, like the purposes of the curriculum, the substance of the curriculum is also negotiable.

THE PRACTICE

The third major dimension of the Curriculum Matrix is *practice*. Unlike purpose and substance, teaching practice is not negotiable. The details of teaching practice are the same everywhere, though in some cultures and among some teachers, some of these details may be omitted or ignored.

In the matrix, nine aspects of practice are named. Each of them is inevitably present in what a teacher and students do, although some receive far more attention than others, and some suffer widespread distortion. We shall consider them briefly. Several of them are not well understood. The nine elements of practice are as follows: *Who* is the student? *What* shall the offering to this student be? *Why* should it be encountered? *How* shall the student encounter it? *When* should a given substance (or subject) be offered? In what *circumstances*, under what *governance*, and at what *cost*? How shall the student's performance be *evaluated* (and by whom)?

Each of these elements of practice is enormously complex. Nevertheless, each of them is always a part of the teaching situation, even when it is ignored.

Who Is the Student?

As teachers, we very often ignore the special character of each person before us, although it is obvious that students differ and that each of them has an individual profile of talents, needs, physical abilities, and so on. We can say all of this, but instead of dealing with individual patterns, we group students according to some criterion (very often, verbal skill), thus stereotyping them, and then teach toward the stereotype. We plead "class management" when such grouping is called into question, and there is no doubt that classes larger than eight or ten students are extremely difficult to manage if one tries to treat the students as individuals. Moreover, very little is known about how to individualize instruction. We use glib terms such as *learning style* to describe the differences among individuals, but the terms have never been defined well enough to enable a teacher to discover what this means within an individual. What, exactly, would we need to know to fit the curriculum to each individual? Nobody knows. The unfortunate result of ignoring individuality is that students tend to believe the stereotypes assigned to them.

What Experiences Should the Student Have?

Equally mysterious is the answer to the question "what experience should an individual student have?" Since we do not know how to discover the individuality of the student, we do not really know what experiences the student should have. Consequently, students love or hate school subjects for largely unknown reasons.

Instead, we rely on the culture as a determiner. The culture says that people need to read, write, and do mathematics, so we show them how to do these things. In addition, we are convinced that people should know some history, some science, and some arts, though we allow far more variation in these fields than we do in the skills of the three R's. Because most students leave the lower schools for employment, we offer some vocational skills as preparation. For the minority who seek further education, we sometimes offer variations on the usual school subjects. This is what is done in the United States. In other countries, and in other cultures, the offering is somewhat different. The important thing to bear in mind is that the experiences we offer in school are determined with very little, if any, attention to the nature of individual students or to the question, "Who is each student?"

Why Experience It?

For teachers, one of our most neglected areas of thought has been understanding the purpose of what we teach. In the elementary grades, it is often said that the purpose of instruction is to prepare the student for the next grade. But that is certainly not a reason that arises from the substance itself. The best reason to learn to read is so that one may partake of reading, of whatever kind. The same thing may be said of writing and mathematics. Geography is learned in order to know one's orientation in the world, and to understand how the Earth's surface may be used and is used by human beings.

But students don't know these reasons for study. They believe (and rightly so, unfortunately) that the reason for study is to pass tests and gain entrance into the next step of the educational system. One goes to school, according to those in charge, to earn high grades. Gaining an education appears to be incidental.

The answer to the question "Why?" is always in the possession of the student. The answer may be, and usually is, disconnected from the reason the experience was offered in the first place. The value of education is not to be found in the symbols of achievement, but in achievement itself. It is not surprising that students often confuse the symbol with the reality.

It follows that the answers to such questions as "Why do I study?" and "Why am I in school?" must be worked out, with help, by each student individually. Their answers will reflect the degree of their maturity. "To get to the next step in school" is the most childish, and earliest, answer. "To get a high grade" is scarcely better. "To get a job" is a bit more meaningful, but it ignores a great part of what is offered or required. The answer most students will give, if they are courageous enough to be candid, is "because somebody says I must." (No wonder teachers spend so much time and imagination making school palatable!) As things stand, students have to answer that basic question for themselves, unaided. It is not surprising that their answers are usually childish; after all, they are children. Teachers and parents have the task of helping children and young people achieve the most competent answers available to the question "Why?"

How Shall it Be Experienced?

The question "How?" concerns the ways school experience shall be undertaken. There was a time when methods courses were a prominent, even basic, part of teacher education. That is no longer the case, unfortunately. Now teachers are largely left to their own devices to work out methods of teaching. Although there are numerous articles and books that deal with motivation, presentation, unifying subjects, evaluation, and the like, no organized way of teaching exists, and most teachers find through trial and error what works for them. For example, some teachers discover the art of mentoring, or coaching, students. Mentoring receives little attention in the professional literature.

Even less is known about how students should undertake learning. Students receive very little help, and they, too, work it out for themselves. There are also some well-known tricks-of-the-trade, such as drill or repetition of key terms or phrases. Many students are acquainted with drill, and they learn through memorization. What they do not learn for themselves is problem-solving. There are students, even at prestigious colleges, who will tell you that they memorized their way through school.

The alternative, rarely employed, is to view all of one's instruction as attempts to help students "make" the subject in the way that a given field requires. One "makes" History by interpreting original records. One "makes" Mathematics by inventing paradigms. One "makes" Literature by inventing it, and also by analyzing good literature the way the best critics do and have done. One "makes" Science by inventing answers to scientific questions and, sometimes, by undertaking to discover something about the nature of things. The same attitude can be brought to the learning of such vocational skills as working with a word processor—not merely by asking the question "How does it work?" but the questions "How did it come to be?" and "Can I improve on it?"; not merely by memorizing the number combinations and calculating them on a computer, but in undertaking the process of inventing the combinations themselves, as if one had never heard, say, of division. Dewey said that you learn what you do. Here, we say that you learn what you make.

When Shall it Be Offered?

Teachers will immediately seek to relate the curriculum to the student's developmental age. Six-year-olds and twelve-year-olds differ, of course, in a great many ways. With respect to the curriculum, however, it is the difference in accumulated experience that matters most. It follows that the answer to the question "When?" should be contained within an appraisal of the student's relevant experience. The appraisal can take the form of an interview, a self-assessment, an evaluation instrument, or some combination of these and other appraisal approaches. What is sought is information concerning the student's skills and knowledge, the attitudes toward the proposed experience, and the student's recall of relevant personal history, especially memories of "making" in the area being considered.

Given this information, it is likely that the answer to the "When?" question will seem evident. The chief difficulty in a classroom will arise from the differences among individuals. One student will be ready for one thing, another for something else. Assignments and suggestions will, therefore, differ from student to student. The class management problem thus created can be partially solved by forming cooperative teams of students. Usually, however, it is attacked through ability grouping, which runs the severe risk of stereotyping young people to their detriment. Instead, a cooperative group can be asked to carry on an assessment of one another's relevant skills, information, and attitudes, and to attempt to suggest appropriate assignments.

Educational literature and textbooks are full of prescriptions for students of different ages. If, instead of ages, we try to relate suggested activities to developmental matters, we will avoid the common problem that arises from inappropriate assignment of learning tasks. Unfortunately, our customs and our language are impediments in this field. There is no such thing as third grade Math, for example, except in teachers' minds, the language of parents, and school texts. The notion of graded subject matter is the product of a serious error perpetuated by educational tradition. The rigid practice that this tradition leads to accounts for a large part of school failure.

The answer to the "When?" question is, therefore, "It depends on the relevant aspects of the individual student's development."

In What Circumstances? Where? Materials?

The circumstances within which school activity takes place include the setting—how much space and availability of special facilities such as a library and a laboratory—and the materials available to teachers—books, paper, audio-visual equipment and materials, and computers. The purposes around which this discussion is organized do not, of themselves, require any circumstances in particular, but organized experiences may well have such requirements. The circumstances are the practical requirements, and planning for curriculum experiences demands that they be taken into account.

Under What Governance?

It makes a great deal of difference whether the curriculum decisions are made at the point of action or elsewhere. In general, the farther away authority is from the immediate instructional situation, the more it should be concerned with policy, and the closer the decision maker is to the point of action, the more the decision should be concerned with practice. School-board members have to learn that distinction; they are advised to avoid micromanaging the school. The distinction between policy and practice is often difficult to discern. For example, state legislatures have been known to mandate reading methods.

When remote authority mandates practice, practice becomes ceremonial and rigid. When a political or religious group mandates what can be read or not read in the classroom, the curriculum always becomes sterile, because teachers become more concerned with what to avoid than with what to do, and imaginativeness takes flight.

In general, the distinction between policy and practice is the distinction between what and how. Noneducators should decide what shall be offered in school in general terms; teachers and especially students must determine how it shall be encountered and the details of what shall be included. Both policy and practice are bound by the purposes to be served.

At What Cost?

The cost of instruction includes not only money, but also time and staff. If there is no time for an activity, or if there is not enough time, either it will not be offered or its quality will suffer. Also, if you cannot staff it, you cannot teach it. Staffing has very often been overlooked in the enthusiasm for an offering. A particular school wanted to maintain a music program but assumed that anyone could teach it. The program died. The core curriculum disappeared in many places because it could not be staffed with appropriately competent teachers. The practical necessities of money, time, and staff must always be met, or the program will fail.

Evaluated How and By Whom?

It is basic to a good education that the student learn to evaluate his or her own efforts and their consequences. This ability is what makes it possible for students to carry on learning after they have left formal education. The importance of this learning by students cannot be overemphasized.

However, self-evaluation is widely ignored. Students learn that teachers will evaluate their work, largely through tests and graded papers. This dependence is so thoroughly a part of their school experience that it seldom occurs to them that they should be able to judge for themselves the adequacy of their efforts. Yet one of the basic lessons of adult life is to know when you are finished with something. It is childish to depend on someone else for that judgment, and employers who deny evaluation to employees soon lose the best of them.

How should this be done? Different categories of school experience require different approaches. In general, the liberal arts—History, Literature, the Arts, and Social studies—are best evaluated when students attempt to interpret or analyze them. Tests limited to factual knowledge are seriously insufficient, though factual knowledge is needed. When so limited, such tests distort the field they seek to measure. The fact that the general public is ignorant of this and therefore takes the knowledge of places to be geography, dates and events to be history, and plots and characters to be literature, simply reflects the widespread deficiencies in this arena that have characterized its schooling.

Evaluation of each experience area ought itself to be the object of systematic attention in school. Inasmuch as intelligent behavior is always goal-directed and successful learning is always the goal of classroom activity, it is only sensible that the goal be discussed early in the classroom experience. The question to raise is "What would convince me that I have succeeded?"

In this chapter, the Curriculum Matrix has been introduced. It is worth emphasizing again that every element in the matrix is itself highly complicated and that all the parts and subparts interact independently. The student's physical self, for example, interacts with every part of classroom practice. The aesthetic self interacts with every school subject, including Math, and also with a student's social behavior. The whole affair is in motion.

Although I have tried to indicate the nature of the principal parts of the matrix, the descriptions of these parts are necessarily incomplete, as readers may have noticed. This incompleteness will persist throughout the remainder of this book, for we are attempting a very large task—to examine how the curriculum would seem if it were organized around the general purpose of achieving humanness. The intention here is to illustrate the possibilities in the curriculum field well enough to suggest how an actual teacher might fill out the discussion.

We begin with an examination of how the transcendent aspect of the self might be brought to awareness in math, where one doesn't expect to find it, and then in the other usual school subjects.

CHAPTER 2

The Transcendent Self

The experience of transcendence, or the sense of one's self as a part of a vastly larger whole, is not generally acknowledged in education. An occasional teacher brings it about, but since it is a private experience, and rare among students, the teacher cannot know that it has taken place unless the student reveals it.

Consequently, it is rarely discussed in educational literature. Maslow (1971) called it the "peak experience," (pp. 170–171) a name that has received widespread use in the literature, but little attention in curriculum design. Bloom (1981, pp. 195–199) described a small inquiry at the University of Chicago in which his students found a handful of graduate students who said that they had undergone such an experience in school. Other inquiries have come close but have not dealt with the experience itself.

An illustration may help.

I was with a busload of sightseers in Rome. We stopped at an elegant small church to admire the building. At one side of the altar, and a bit to the rear of it, was Michelangelo's *Moses*. I was transfixed. The statue suddenly became my entire universe. I lost all sense of time and place. I was utterly absorbed. Moses glared in rage at his people; the tablet fell from his hands. Having just come from God, he was undergoing the shock of human frailty. For me, the experience transcended the place, the craft of the sculptor, the fact that, after all, I was looking at stone. I felt somehow enlarged.

I do not know how long I stood there. When I came back to my senses, the touring group had left, and I was alone. The majesty, the awesome presence, and the intensity of that moment have remained with me to this day.

THE TRANSCENDENT EXPERIENCE

I finally found an extensive literature on transcendence under the heading *spiritual*. This literature was written by theologians, whom the psychologists and other social scientists seem to have ignored. What, according to the theologians, is the nature of the transcendent experience? What does it signify? What is its source? I received some help from acquaintances who are theologians, and began a fascinating excursion into their literature, which I read with my mind on just one thing: What is the transcendent, or spiritual, experience?

In essence, the theologians had found what Maslow and Bloom reported—had found it earlier and had found much more. According to them, the experience is universal and ancient. Mankind has always been overwhelmed by the wonder of the life process—birth, growth, death. Primitive societies have marveled at the enormous, often hostile, forces of nature and at the mysteries of the sky above.

People have responded to this kind of awareness in many ways—through ritual, supplication, religion, art objects, the emphasis and subordination of habits and feelings (such as celebrations and taboos)—often in search of ecstasy, or transforming experiences. The literature of the world's great religions is full of testimony to this fact, and it has found repeated expression in secular literature.

The idea of the transcendent or spiritual begins with awe, or fear. Nature is viewed as essentially hostile, as in Beowulf's encounter with Grendel, which is usually understood to be a metaphor for man's struggle with nature. In both Norse and Greek mythology, a capricious, hostile nature was personified in gods and spirits—such as Thor, Apollo, Vulcan, and Loki—who had to be feared and placated. Otto (1923, p. 59) calls this fear "daemonic dread."

The fear was expressed in aesthetic statements in every form, from idols and edifices to drama and music, as the great religious traditions took shape. What had begun as fear became almost overwhelming wonder, astonishment, even amazement, at the nature of things. It came to influence mankind's sense of existence.

Existence was viewed as essentially dimensional. Man dwelled on Earth; there was a space between Earth and Heaven, where dwelled the demons; there was Heaven, which was beyond comprehension, where dwelled the gods. Early man saw the general in the particular—all of terror in a lion—much as Blake and Wordsworth did in their time—the universe in a grain of sand, or in a daffodil. As H. Smith (1982, p. 41) says, "The terrestrial plane proceeds from and is explained by the intermediate, the intermediate by the celestial, and the celestial by the infinite."

The dimensional, spherical shape of the universe was made manifest in many ways. Marshall McLuhan once pointed out to me that the cathedral contained for the medieval person a sphere of experience. When one was inside the building, all the most significant aspects of the world came

at one from all directions simultaneously. The Earth-centered cosmology
of that time was also spherical. Earth was at the center of a series of spheres,
the lesser contained in the greater, from which the lesser derived its meaning. The whole system was believed to be in perfect balance.

I discern two basic elements of the transcendent or spiritual experience in this account: the experience of dread or awe or fearfulness (later,
wonder) and the experience of connectedness with something greater than
what immediately appears. The latter is ordinarily called "transcendence,"
which is the term I have adopted for this aspect of the self.

Other terms have gathered around the idea. Otto (1923, p. 60) calls
it the "wholly other," Tillich (1959, p. 41) the "ground of being" or the
"unconditioned," in which one deals with matters of "ultimate concern."
"Ritual," according to Jones (1973, p. 16), "derives its energy and focus
from the transcendent present in the individual or community consciousness or belief." Phenix (1964, p. 61) says, "The term *transcendence* refers
to the sense of limitless going beyond any given state or realization
of being." He points to "cognate" terms: *spirit, infinitude, idealization.*
He continues by indicating how the idea of transcendence compares
with Dewey's notion of the continuous progressive reconstruction of
experience.

Bloom's (1981, pp. 195–199) students, mentioned at the beginning
of this chapter, reported a loss of the sense of time and place that is analo-
gous to my experience with the Michelangelo. "The learning experience became the figure, while the ground . . . disappeared." The Chicago students saw the experience as immediately true in a fundamental
way and as one in which "organizing, analytic, and application types of
thinking were temporarily suspended." The experience for them was
"awe-inspiring," "wonderful."

The students speak the same way the theologians do. The experience is awesome; it goes beyond ordinary reason; it is fundamental—a
moment of immediate truth—or, as Phenix and many others would have
it, transcendent.

The theologians claim that the transcendent experience is latent in
mankind and can be awakened in everyone. It is a sudden awareness of
the connection between what is immediately apparent and a vastly larger
sphere of being. This experience may be evoked, or called out.

This flash of awareness corresponds with Maslow's (1968, p. 169)
reports about his clients. He calls it "an illumination, a revelation, an
insight, that leads to the cognition of being." Unlike the theologians, Maslow
distinguishes between the people he calls "self-actualizing" (i.e., fully
mature and internally organized) and others. The self-actualized have frequent peak experiences; others have them rarely or not at all.

These sudden awakenings are sometimes seen in the theological tradition as mystic visions. Mystics have reported them since the earliest times. I conclude that mysticism arises from a self-immolating encounter with ultimate reality—not unlike the experience of one who climbs out of Plato's cave, sees the source of all light, and is temporarily blinded. Sometimes mysticism is expressed in poetry, as in Blake's "Tyger," which not only expresses the awe and wonder of the experience but also seeks to awaken it in us.

The idea of the transcendent or spiritual thus seems to have a scope, from daemonic dread or awe, at one extreme, to mystic expression, at the other. The term includes this entire range of meanings in our time; it has shed none. The only new idea associated with it is Otto's (1923, p. 60) "numinous," which "can only be incited, induced, and aroused" or, in Maslow's language, "triggered."

It is interesting that neither the theologians nor Maslow attempt to develop a concept of the experience they call the "transcendent," or "spiritual," or "peak experience." They seek only to assert its reality. The idea seems to exist in a cloud of meaning, not as a concept. It is a "state of mind, . . . purely felt experience, only to be indicated symbolically, by ideograms," says Otto (1923, p.70). In this sense it is nonrational, somewhat as music and sculpture are nonrational. The idea goes beyond reason, as Bloom's students implied.

So, what does one do to grasp a cloud? To use reason to examine the nonrational? One way to proceed is to examine the language people use to talk about it. Doing just that, I found that accounts of the transcendent or spiritual or peak experience in the literature I examined fall into three categories that describe the experience itself and two categories that deal with the impact of the experience:

1. The intellectual or what is nonrational or beyond reason—17 occurrences (non-rational, stupefying, ultimate meaning, unimaginable, boundless)
2. The transcendent or the sense of going beyond—15 occurrences (transcendent, being unlimited, tropism of the soul toward the universe)
3. The mystic—6 occurrences (mystic vision, sublime, reverence, exultation)
4. The impact as a whole—45 occurrences (awesome, singular experience, timeless, spaceless, overpowering, nonvoluntary, astonishing)
5. The impact in detail—18 occurrences (inner illumination, wonder, amazing, of great moment, loss of fear)

As Kaufman (in Buber, 1970, p. 140 n.) says of Buber: "Such writers seem less concerned with precise denotation than with rich connections and associations."

Of these categories, the first two—the intellectual and the transcendent—appear essentially cognitive in character, as if the transcendent experience begins in the mind. It does not. It begins as a kind of assault on one's sense of existence. The assault is in some part intellectual, but principally it is an assault on pure reason, in which remember, "organizing, analytic, application types of thinking are temporarily suspended" (Bloom, 1981, p. 195). The experience is self-contained. It is not instrumental to anything else.

The aspect of human experience we examine here appears to defy objective analysis, if we are to believe those who have given it the most thought. How, then, shall we approach it? One way is by adopting the method of inquiry used by the theologians and by the clinician, Maslow.

This method takes as its domain the testimony of those who have undergone the experience. Theologians gather this evidence from the history, literature, and artifacts of the principal world religions. Maslow listened to the accounts of his self-actualized clients. Bloom's colleagues interviewed 80 students.

The truth claiming of these scholars rests on verification by the reader. The theologians seem to use the following line of argument:

1. Here is the testimony of the ages—people have spiritual, transcendent experiences.
2. Look in on yourself. Do you not resonate to these accounts?
3. Here is a theory of the origin and significance of the experience as it bears on some classic theological question.

Maslow and Bloom proceed in essentially the same way. They gather testimony from clients, and leave it to their readers to find parallels in their own lives. They then apply what they have found to their real-world preoccupation with education.

The theologians I have consulted are unanimous in rejecting the classic scientific methods used in the social sciences because they judge those methods to be inapplicable to their concern. Even Maslow, who was at one time president of the American Psychological Association, acknowledged that his interest in the peak experience was strange for a scientist. H. Smith (1977) writes about a conversation with a scientist, while he was teaching at the Massachusetts Institute of Technology:

> As so often happened in such circumstances, the conversation turned to the differences between science and the humanities. We were getting nowhere when suddenly he broke in on something I was saying with the authority of a man who has discovered Truth. "I have it!" he exclaimed. "The difference between us is that I count, and you don't!" (p. 11)

Concealed in the scientist's double entendre is a complete lack of under-standing of what people like Smith do.

There is a mounting discussion of the methods of inquiry appropriate to the social and behavioral sciences. There have been whole meetings, and several books, devoted to "qualitative research." Some contemporary mathematicians insist that we recognize the limits of quantitative analysis. To these may be added some theologians, such as Buber (1970), who claims that the "it world" of science fails to admit his "you," or "thou" (p. 100), and Tillich (1959), who insists that different levels of reality require dif-ferent approaches (pp. 56–57). H. Smith (1982), who has devoted much attention to this matter, suggests a strategy:

> In place of the usual tendency to begin with the accepted world and add to it only what collected evidence requires, I am asking if it would harm us to conjure the most interesting world we can and then drop from it what reason erases. There is some resemblance to Anselm's *credo ut intelligam*— "I believe in order to understand" (or better) "I get involved in order to understand". (p. 151)

What, then, is left for those preoccupied with curriculum and teach-ing? I suggest, with Epstein (1981, passim), that great teachers find what is captivating or transcendent about their disciplines and teach from these insights to awaken the transcendent experience in their students. Again, we must remember that the transcendent experience is always private. As teachers, we cannot know if it has taken place unless a student tells us it has. We can only invite it; we cannot bring it about directly. We shall see whether we can find astonishment, or transcendent possibilities, within some of the subjects usually offered in school.

Mathematics

We shall begin with Mathematics, which is, of course, fundamental to our age. The idea that Math has transcendent value seems strange because most of us have thought of it as consisting of a number of memorized paradigms. Thus, to solve a math problem, one need only match the problem with the right paradigm. This may lead to an "aha!", or gestalt, experience, but it can scarcely lead to transcendence.

Where is the possibility of transcendence in Mathematics? Recent lit-erature on Math as one of the humanities suggests that it can be found in Math history, which suggests a redefinition of the field.

According to most mathematicians at this time, Mathematics is rigor-ous thinking. That is what it is, and that is all it is. In offering this definition of their discipline, they are, indeed, true to its history since Euclid. They are also responsible for the widespread phenomenon they call "math anxiety," for the rigorous thinking of mathematics is full of failure for a great many learners.

An emerging view of the field says that it consists of a series of remarkable feats of human imagination—leaps in understanding that make it possible to go beyond what is immediately perceived into a long series of transforming theories about reality. In other words, they make it possible to *transcend* immediate reality, to *go beyond* common sense. The discoveries by mathematicians since ancient times are all of this kind.

The main thing to understand about Mathematics is that it is profoundly *human*. If it is marvelous, and of course it is, it is because human beings are marvelous. It follows that Mathematics can awaken within us an awareness of our own humanity, especially that aspect of it involving imagination. According to Klein (1978),

> The achievements of mathematicians demonstrate the capacity of the human mind, and the exhibition of what human reason can accomplish has given man the courage and confidence to tackle additional seemingly impenetrable mysteries of the cosmos, to seek cures for fatal diseases, and to question and improve the economic and political systems under which people live. (p. 4)

Mathematics is also a *spiritual* enterprise. This is not to say that it is religious. However, like religion, borrowing Tillich's terms, it does address some ultimate questions. For example, in discussing the concept of infinity, Guillen (1983) closes by summarizing where mathematical thought has brought us:

> The physical no longer does contain us wholly, if it ever did. We are beings at once finite and infinite, in the sense that our physical selves are prisoners of a finite realm, but not so our imaginative selves. . . . Now we roam freely beyond the ordinary infinity of the ponderable universe. (p. 181)

In a famous passage, Galileo thought he had found that mathematics is the language of the universe:

> That vast book that stands forever open before our eyes, the universe, cannot be read until we have learned the language and become familiar with the characters in which it is written. It is written in the mathematical language, without which means it is humanly impossible to comprehend a single word. (Jacobs, 1970, p. xii)

Small wonder that a quip popular with some mathematicians is "God is a mathematician." With Klein (1978, p. 1), mathematicians say, "Our world is to a large extent what mathematicians say it is."

Another characteristic of mathematics is that it is *astonishing*. A former student of mine said to me, "When I first heard of negative numbers, at age 12, it blew my mind." Years later her continued enthusiasm for mathematics led her to write an outstanding dissertation in a different field, but one in which she "thought like a mathematician."

Or, in another example, a high school mathematics teacher reported that when she tried to explain the concept of a variable in an equation, a student suddenly exclaimed, "You mean I can put *any* number I want in there? Wow!"

Finally, Mathematics is *majestic,* overwhelmingly powerful. Shafaravich, one of the world's leading researchers on algebraic geometry, concludes:

> A superficial glance at mathematics may give an impression that it is a result of separate individual efforts of many scientists scattered about in continents and in ages. However, the inner logic of its development reminds one much more of the work of a single intellect, developing its thought systematically and consistently, using a variety of human individualities only as a means. (quoted in Davis & Hersh, 1981, pp. 52–54)

The evidence for this conclusion is that mathematicians have made several discoveries, essentially identical, independently, at entirely different times and places. It is as if mathematics arose from a primal need to deal with nature. The ideas from which all mathematics descends, it has been speculated, are the ideas of "more and less," "greater and smaller," and "one and more than one."

We turn from the nature of the field to some ideas within it that have had a transforming effect on the way human beings think. Each of these was an astounding leap of human imagination. Each one is a candidate for awakening the experience of transcendence among students. Each of them serves as an historical milestone that split Mathematics history, in the sense that Math was one thing before each idea and something else afterward. I have located seven such events:

1. *Counting and the Development of Symbols.* Primitive people probably counted things such as their fingers and toes, objects around them, and the like. The other animals, too, could count a little. But imagine the first person who made a mark to represent something! No other animal had ever done that. The first mathematical symbol was probably a tally. Enumeration itself was an imaginative feat, but even greater was the feat of inventing a symbol for an object. Consider the difference between ///// and V, or 5. Later, consider the difference between MCMLXXXIV and 1984. Human beings got beyond the other animals when they first invented symbols to represent groups of objects.

2. *Combining Quantities.* It was a great leap of the imagination for people to go beyond enumerating to combining quantities, as in addition and multiplication. For example, it is difficult to combine quantities using Roman numerals. It was even more difficult for the ancient Egyptians, who could only multiply by 2 (but notice the similarity to our binary computers), or for the Babylonians, who used base 60 (like our clocks). They had to shed a lot of baggage—for example, that certain numbers have religious properties–before the elegant simplicity of the modern decimal system became possible.

3. *The Nature of Proof.* Euclid's *Elements* split mathematics history into two parts: pre- and post-Euclid. His contribution was the idea of proof. Having taken part in the legalistic disputations at the Agora in Athens, he proceeded to demonstrate that from a few self-evident axioms, it was possible to construct a whole apparatus—plane geometry. Euclid's method of proof dominated mathematics for 2,000 years. There was an inexorable certainty to such logic, all the way from the simplest syllogism to the most elaborate construction. For centuries, the force of this logic has led to many a transcendent experience for students of Mathematics. With Plato (trans. 1935, p. 54), they have come to believe that "the knowledge at which geometry aims is the knowledge of the eternal."

4. *Zero and Negative Numbers.* The invention of zero took place independently during the seventh century in China, in India, and among the Mayans. Once one has the concept of zero, it immediately becomes inviting to go up and down from it, into positive and negative numbers. To imagine zero, people had to get rid of the idea that counting always involves some thing or things. They had to toy with the idea that *nothing* is *something*. They must have had at least to think of the distinction (again, made much later) between *nothing* and *nothingness*.

5. *Sets and Infinity.* The idea of infinity remained untamed from ancient Greece to modern times. It defied satisfactory mathematical definition, retaining vague doctrinal meanings. The idea was tamed during the nineteenth century by Cantor, who is well known as the inventor of set theory, now widely taught to young children. Not so widely known is his impact on the idea of infinity. Cantor began by considering sets—of numbers, chairs, orchestras, anything. If the elements of one set could be paired numerically with the elements of another, then the sets were equivalent in size. The definition of a set does not require that the populations of the sets be counted. Any known set can be considered a subset of a still larger set, and that of a still larger set, ad infinitum. Now, Cantor made the leap: Since an infinite set is still a set, it could be thought of as a subset of a still more infinite set, and that of yet another, and so on. All the transfinite numbers and all the subsequent sets go beyond infinity as we have thought of it—"ordinary" infinity, as Cantor called it. The sequence of transfinite

numbers is as boundless as the cosmos. We are faced with an infinity of infinities, a strictly mind-boggling concept. (If it were not mind-boggling, it would still be a subset!) Guillen (1983, p. 48) likens the concept to the idea of infinity as expressed by Kant and St. Gregory, whom he quotes: "No matter how far our mind may have progressed in the contemplation of God, it does not attain to what He is but to what is beneath Him." To take another example, theoretically, we may cut something in half forever without wholly disposing of it. It is like the asymptotic line that forever slopes toward another line but never touches it, or like an airplane that is forever landing but never touches the ground, or like society, or a person, forever seeking perfection but never achieving it.

6. *Space and Time.* The notion of multiple dimensions, or an infinity of dimensions, is one we can say, but we cannot grasp. One of the dimensions, the fourth, is time. Einstein's contribution gave us a new view of the nature of the universe. It consists of complex surfaces such that moving objects change their size. They are subject to not three dimensions but four, including time. Space, it develops, must be thought of as curved. The geometry of Euclid, which describes planes, does not deal with the universe as it is. Einstein was not the first to challenge Euclid; indeed, he relied on his nineteenth century predecessors, who had.

Non-Euclidean geometry is associated with two men: Lobachevsky, and Riemann. Others had come upon essentially the same ideas before Lobachevsky, namely, Bolyai and Gauss. Both demonstrated that a geometry as robust as Euclid's could be constructed, but it would be different. There is an alternative to Euclid's logic, which had been the only logic since ancient times. Riemann's geometry conceives of the mathematical world as a sphere, in which a straight line is like the arc of a great circle. Straight lines do not stretch to infinity, as in Euclid. The ends of a straight line eventually meet.

These difficult, mind-boggling ideas have transformed not only Mathematics but also one's sense of where one is in the scheme of things. They certainly are candidates for evoking the experience of transcendence.

7. *Uncertainty and Faith.* The work of Gödel, which surfaced in 1931 and has withstood a rigorous examination by the Mathematics community, deals with the basic structures of Mathematics. It requires the introduction of uncertainty into a field that had above all been certain that it was dealing with incontrovertible truth. It defies the belief in pure logic that until then had been the glory of the field. Hilbert, early in the twentieth century in Germany, claimed that anything at all could be understood mathematically, given sufficient rigor, talent, and persistence. (We educators are reminded of the dictum attributed to Thorndike at about the same time: "Anything that exists, exists in some degree, and can be measured.")

Gödel's genius is that he uses logic to demonstrate the limits of logic. "In any mathematical system rich enough to include number theory," he says (Stein, 1969, p. 351), "there is an expression expressible within the system that is true, yet is not provable within the system." The method is deceptively simple. Gödel considers an hypothesis such as this: "Using logic, this hypothesis cannot be proved true." That hypothesis can be proved either way. Since it can, one must suppose it to be true. Tricky! Guillen (1983) calls such statements, of which many can be made, "unprovable verities." But if something is true but cannot be proven, one must accept it on faith. Faith! The word is anathema to formal mathematicians, such as the followers of Hilbert.

This discussion on uncertainty must also include the recent work on chaos, which deals with the strictly unpredictable, such as the weather over a long term, or the behavior of a single drop of water in a waterfall. There is an ultimate, but strange, order to such chaos.

These seven ideas and others of their power suggest that the study of mathematics can become exciting, unforgettable, even transforming and transcendent, because such study takes us out of our restricted environments into unlimited freedom of thought and imagination. Thus, we can come to see ourselves differently. However, there are prerequisites, two of which are becoming evident. They are requirements of practice.

The first of these is *immersion.* Ideas of this sort do not burst out on the uninformed. As Noddings and Shore (1984) point out, in Mathematics we begin with a puzzle of some kind, then carry on the necessary study and drill to get the tools for dealing with it firmly within our grasp, where-upon the solution may (or may not) come suddenly; we just *might* have the experience of transcendence. That experience cannot take place in a vacuum.

The second is *time to think,* a prerequisite often denied in the classroom. Experiments with "wait time" found that most teachers expect immediate answers to their constant questions. If they wait as little as five seconds (preferably more), the quality of the response improves dramatically.

Having considered the possibility of the transcendent experience in Mathematics at some length—because it seemed an unlikely subject for a transcendent experience—let us now consider that possibility in some other school subjects, which seem more likely to invite the experience.

Social Studies or History

The experience of transcendence is possible at several points in the teaching of Social Studies or History. There are, of course, great transforming events, such as the discovery of the New World or the account of Marco Polo's travels, which opened up whole new views of human culture and existence. The idea of human culture itself could become a transforming experience.

Perhaps the most readily available concept in the teaching of History is the idea of time, coupled with the idea of History itself. The understanding that the present constantly becomes part of the past and that all of us are ourselves historical figures can loom large in one's experience. Perhaps some students will begin to keep daily journals understanding that such journals are part of the record that may later be studied historically. Such a realization could be dramatic for some students. In any case, it would deepen one's understanding of the nature of History as the interpretation of what remains from the past, or the record.

Science

The possibility of a transcendent experience is almost everywhere in Science. In the physical sciences, there is the wonder of microscopic order. In the life sciences, there are the universality and the mystery of life itself in its seemingly infinite manifestations. In Astronomy, there are the phenomenon of infinite space and questions like "What came before the Big Bang?" Science is full of mystery and wonder.

Literature

Even mediocre literature, such as jingles, Robert Service poems, or trivial fiction, seeks to create worlds that we can inhabit imaginatively. When one gets beyond plot, characters, rhyme, meter, and dates to the actual substance of literature, the worlds made available can, and often do, have an enlarging effect on the reader. Once one has read *Huckleberry Finn*, for example, and drifted down the Mississippi with Huck and Jim, that nineteenth-century world lives as part of one's self. Once one has really confronted a great lyric poem, such as "The Ode to the West Wind," one can see one's self as part of nature. Great literature can have a transforming effect, if it is encouraged or even simply allowed.

Vocational Subjects

The temptation in the vocational subjects is to limit them to the marketable skills. Obviously, such skills are at the heart of the teaching about computers, auto repair, woodworking, or electronics, not to mention the many others. If instruction in these fields concentrates solely on skill development for later employment, the opportunity for a transcendent experience is severely limited, if not lost.

To broaden the importance of vocational subjects—to make them a respected part of general education—one needs only to put them in a proper context. Computer skills are used for the highly significant human activities of analysis and communication. What makes analysis human? Communication? Communication has a design, an artistry, of its own. If those questions receive serious attention, the skills associated with them will acquire an importance that goes far beyond job holding. Students can be invited to take their own being, or humanity, seriously, because the vocational skills will be seen in their broad human context.

The Arts

The more serious art expressions are often intended both to express and to evoke a transcendent experience. At their best, the great masterpieces of painting, sculpture, opera, symphonic music, dance, literature, and drama all share this quality. What is often overlooked is that popular music and dance, too, are sometimes intended to evoke such an experience, though not by the name "transcendent." When one views enormous crowds of young people gyrating to the music of a popular performer, one must understand that these young people are seeking to become "lost" in the experience. At the same time, they undoubtedly feel themselves part of a much larger entity—the enormous crowd, the other young people not present.

The border between the transcendent experience and the aesthetic experience is difficult to draw. We turn now to the aesthetic self, and the difference will become apparent. We shall first examine its presence at some length in an unlikely place, History, and then in some other school subjects.

CHAPTER 3

The Aesthetic Self

Like the transcendent self, the aesthetic self is largely ignored in schooling. The term is generally associated with the arts, which in philistine American society are considered mere entertainment, to be indulged in only when all the other requirements of daily living have been met. The universality and the power of aesthetic experience, while always present, are generally ignored.

Not here. Here, we shall see how aesthetic considerations operate in the teaching of the usual school subjects, especially History. First, though, we must deal with the term *aesthetics* itself.

The aesthetic dimension of human development—indeed, of humanness itself—is universal. It is an essential aspect of the self. It may be neglected, but it enters inevitably into our view of our personal worth and into the making of all kinds of decisions (e.g., by asking the question "How will it look?"). The portrayal of national events in the popular press, for example, is dominated by such aesthetic considerations as their dramatic quality (as contrasted with their general importance), the appearance of people in photographs, and the language chosen for headlines. These were headlines on the front page of the *New York Times* of October 18, 1997: "Little Panel That Could, Did, Posing Threat of Trade War," "Africa Finds Old Borders Are Eroding," and "Trimming More Pork." Alternatives to these editorial choices might be thought "dull," an aesthetic term. Inasmuch as aesthetic considerations dominate the selection of matters to be discussed by journalists, we are led from one dramatic sensation to another—from the tragic destruction of a famous football player's family to a sensational murder, to the depiction of the national election as a race. Political debates are treated as art forms; the issues are subordinated.

Knowledge of the aesthetic dimension of human awareness often separates leaders from followers, not only in politics but also in business, in academia, in the professions, and in the trades. Ignorance of the aesthetic accounts for all kinds of human failures, from the personal to the societal. The universality and the overlooked importance of the aesthetic are reasons to search for it throughout the school curriculum. Thus, we shall examine what the term *aesthetic* means and how it appears and may be considered in school education.

THE AESTHETIC EXPERIENCE

Webster's Collegiate Dictionary defines *aesthetics* as "a branch of philosophy dealing with the beautiful and with judgments concerning beauty." Thus I turn to the philosophers and the art critics for their ideas.

Croce (1909/1983) and others warn against the misuse of analysis. It is tempting to believe that we have found the essence of something by taking it apart. This has led some critics to conduct dissections instead of analysis. A ridiculous example would be a chemical analysis of the paint in a painting or a grammatical analysis of a poem, as if such an analysis would reveal the aesthetic value of the work.

But some analysis is valuable for it helps to bring our aesthetic experience to consciousness. It is important, however, to avoid confusing the aesthetic response with scientific analysis, or more generally, confusing art and science. The fact that aesthetic experience is universal and can exist in science does not mean that scientific analysis is the same as aesthetic analysis. Of course, some scientific formulations have aesthetic value. $E = mc^2$ is an "elegant" statement, but elegant, an aesthetic quality, refers to the exact fit, the parsimonious quality of the statement, not to the scientific process that led up to it. Some scientific processes are "beautiful," but the criteria used to reach that judgment have to do with scientific truth, not the truth of the arts. Both science and the arts lead to their own forms of truth, but each exists within strict boundaries. Scientific truth depends on rational demonstration and it stops there. Truth in art depends on the quality of the aesthetic experience it evokes, which we shall examine here. The examination of the boundaries between science and art has commanded the attention of philosophers, especially during the twentieth century.

For the purposes of this discussion, it is sufficient to understand the aesthetic response, or experience. Some of those who have written about aesthetics are helpful here. Beardsley (1981, pp. 9–10), for example, in describing the aesthetic experience writes: "It involves attention to a portion of a phenomenally objective field, an awareness of form and of such qualities as beauty, elegance, grace, dignity, frivolity, and irony; it has a high degree of coherence and completeness; it is intrinsically satisfying." This calls to mind the end of Keats's "Ode on a Grecian Urn": "'Beauty is truth, truth beauty.'" Beardsley's "intrinsically satisfying" is a statement of the nature of aesthetic truth.

The most widely mentioned reference on the aesthetic experience is Dewey's (1934/1980) *Art as Experience*. There, Dewey does two things important to educators: he discusses the concept of *experience*, which is absolutely fundamental to an understanding of the developments in education since his time, and he sets forth directly the nature of aesthetic experience. Hear him on the universality of the aesthetic experience, Dewey (1934/1980, pp. 5–6) writes, "The arts which today have vitality for the average person are things he does not take to be arts: for instance, the movie, jazzed music, the comic strip, and too frequently, newspaper accounts of love-nests, murders, and episodes of bandits." He might have added, school textbooks and many other assigned readings as well.

Next, Dewey turns to the nature of experience. He equates it with life itself; living creatures interact with their environments and it is the interaction that is experience: "Experience is the result, the sign, and the reward of the interaction of organism and environment which, when it is carried to the full, is a transformation of interaction into participation and communication" (1934/1980, p. 22).

If experience is *inter*action, then telling, in whatever form, is not of itself teaching. If one learns what one does, or better, if one learns what one makes of what one has acquired, then college lectures are not, by themselves, teaching; they are preliminaries to the actual learning. Obviously, thinking or any form of "making" requires information and skill, but information and skill are only preliminaries. By themselves, they are "merely academic." As Dewey says in many places, experience is a matter of both doing and undergoing; acts have consequences that lead to further acts, which also have consequences. Experience is serial, reflexive, and ongoing. Things happen, we take them in, we make a response, which leads to further experience. Teachers are mainly concerned with students' experiences, so conceived.

What makes an experience aesthetic? Dewey's (1934/1980, p. 50) answer is, "That which distinguishes an experience as esthetic is conversion of resistance and tensions, of excitations that in themselves are temptations to diversion, into a movement into an inclusive and fulfilling close."

The key comment here is at the end of the statement: "a movement toward an inclusive and fulfilling close." With Beardsley (1981) and others, and borrowing from Ross Mooney (in conversation), we may call this a "feeling of fit." For Dewey and others, this feeling arises from the success of the *form* of the object, whatever it may be. For Dewey (1934/1980, p. 81), "[T]he *form* of the whole is therefore present in every member. Fulfilling, consummating, are continuous functions, not mere ends, located in one place only."

Dewey's "elements," or "components," differ from one art to another. Form is different in dance, painting, opera, poetry, and so on. A particular kind of prose writing is the form we shall examine in this chapter. First, however, there are other elements of the aesthetic experience to consider.

Dewey (1934/1980, p. 61) warns us not to confuse the feeling of consummation or fulfillment with emotion, with mere gush, which leads to "the error—which has unfortunately invaded esthetic theory—of supposing that the mere giving way to an impulsion, native or habitual, constitutes expression. . . . Emotional discharge is a necessary, but not a sufficient, condition of expression."

Music may bring tears to the eyes, or a great sculpture may fill one with awe, or tragedy may make us feel pity and terror. These emotional responses are evidence of the impact of an aesthetic experience, but they are neither the whole of it nor are they necessarily significant parts of it.

It is worth reemphasizing that we may consider anything at all aesthetically, and we do. As Arnstine (1970, p. 32) says, "Anything which, when attended to in the proper way, can lead us to the satisfaction . . . outlined here, can be an aesthetic experience."

Some objects of our attention offer richer aesthetic experience than do others. Some may even be not beautiful, but ugly. Aesthetic experience ranges from the sublime to the unspeakable. To characterize something as tasteless or magnificent, trite or imaginative, grotesque or beautifully formed, is to report our aesthetic experience. Aesthetically, objects may be offensive or shocking or inspirational or moving; all of these terms are reports of our aesthetic experience. It is worth noting that we use that sort of language all the time; we report aesthetically almost constantly.

Now let us consider art criticism, which is largely concerned with aesthetic judgment, or critical analysis. Great critics, such as Lionel Trilling or Edmund Wilson, make their aesthetic experience public. They explain it, thus providing reaches of experience not otherwise available to us. They examine many kinds of objects, including some the rest of us would ignore. Some contemporary artists, for example, apparently intend to compel us to attend to the commonplace, for there is wonder to be found there. Some seem to intend merely to surprise us or even to shock us. Such work is to be considered according to its kind.

"The Shooting of Dan McGrew" by Robert Service is good for its kind; so is Shelley's "Ode to the West Wind." To compare the two poems by the same criterion would be pointless. However, the Shelley poem is more likely to repay prolonged attention than the Service poem. The kind—category or context—of work determines how it is to be experienced—how we are to approach it.

We must therefore begin by placing the work in its appropriate category, or context. The first question is, what kind of thing is this? Is this kind rewarding to attend to? How fruitful is it likely to be to consider this as a work of art? If it is a bit of writing, how shall it be approached: as a newspaper account? as fiction? as a primary document, such as the Declaration of Independence or Anne Frank's diary?

There are other questions. As Dewey (1934/1980, p. 90) says, an artist "resees" what is portrayed, whatever the medium. Similarly, observers in some sense participate in the making of the object. If we have tried to play the piano, we "hear into" the performance of a great pianist, somewhat like a fellow performer. The same can be said about writing, about acting in a drama, and so on. If we know something of the skills entailed in producing the object, our aesthetic experience is enhanced. So the second question is, how did the object come to be, technically?

Third, how does the work appeal to us? Take the word *appeal* in its literal sense: how does the work call out to us for corroboration or response? The appeal in the arts is often to the senses, such as seeing, hearing, or tasting. It can even be kinesthetic. In written prose, the appeal is to our sensed experience. Winston Churchill called the first volume of his World War II history *The Gathering Storm*, presumably to appeal to our experience of threat, as from a violent storm.

The fourth question arises from Dewey's term, *expression*. What does the work express? For Dewey (1934/1980, Chap. 4), the answer involves a calling up of relevant personal experience—all of it—and a matching of that experience with the art work. Expression differs from appeal in that the appeal is directly to our senses, but expression is a property of the art work itself: the work expresses something. What it expresses we may take to be its aesthetic truth. This truth will vary from one of us to another, depending on our personal experience. For each of us, the encounter of our personal past and our present yields our individual aesthetic truth.

One's encounter with these questions may yield an emotional response, and the emotion may well be what one remembers later. But as we have noticed earlier, emotion is not the main thing, nor is it the whole of the aesthetic experience. The expression of an art work is a complex of emotion, intellect, and recalled experience. The term expression means both impact and aesthetic truth.

Borrowing from Broudy (1975, pp. 11–12) we may summarize the four aspects of the aesthetic experience as the following questions:

1. What *kind* of work is this? (Do I admire this kind?)
2. What is its *form*? (How do the elements fit together?)

3. How do I *sense* it? (What is its appeal?)
4. What does it *express*? (What is its aesthetic truth, its impact?)

The Social Studies/History

Consider the writing of history, a field not usually associated with the aesthetic component of the self. What is history? It is easier to see what it is not than what it is; what it is not is a study of the past. The first thing to understand about the past is that it is gone. Historians study, not the past, but what remains from the past in the present—the record, in all its forms. The record is always incomplete; what historians make of it changes as the record changes. Historians always interpret the record. Their interpretations always reflect their strengths as historiographers, their biases, their talents as writers, and their limitations. Here, we shall concentrate on their talents as writers, for it is the aesthetic quality of their writing that makes it memorable and that has impact on students.

All historians are concerned with the quality of their writing. Those who are not, whose concern is entirely with the accuracy of the record, are not historians; they are archivists. (One of the relevant criticisms of much school testing of students is that it tests archivism, not history.)

Some of the interpretations have a grandeur that has aesthetic impact. Arnold Toynbee (1960) is generally considered to be one of the great historians of our time. His conception of his own work is grand indeed:

> Why do people study History? The present writer's personal answer would be that an historian, like anyone else who has had the happiness of having an aim in life, has found his vocation in a call from God to "feel after Him and find Him." . . . [The historian has a] vision of God's creative activity on the move in a frame. . . . The historical angle of vision shows us the physical cosmos moving centrifugally in a four-dimensional frame of life-time-space, and it shows us Spirit, moving through a fateful exercise of their spiritual freedom, moving either towards their Creator or away from Him. (p. 908)

Other historians have had different grand conceptions. Braudel, the great French historian, chose to write about whole regions, such as the Mediterranean; Parkinson saw U.S. history as the conquering of the frontier; Gibbon wrote about the decline and fall, not the whole story, of the Roman Empire. The interpretation of the record can be grand or narrow, inspiring or pedestrian. All of these characterizations are aesthetic terms.

Of course, there is much more to history than its aesthetic qualities. Historiography deals with the adequacy and accuracy of historical accounts. Our concern here, though, is with the aesthetic quality of the writing, because that is what determines much of its impact on students and other readers. Written History is, after all, literature, whether well or poorly done.

A simple formula exists to consider the aesthetic impact of a piece of literature. It involves three qualities of writing that, depending on how well they fit one another, may jointly lead to an aesthetic impact. The three are *form*, *style*, and *content*. When writing of great events, if that is the content, an author uses a special form, a narrative, in which smaller events lead to a climax, which is somehow resolved (often, tragically). The style the author adopts is sometimes called "high seriousness," with evocative language—no puns, no jokes, no trivialities. The content dictates both the form and the style. In the degree that the three fit, the writing is aesthetically successful.

Consider, for example, several school history texts and their treatment of a fairly obscure event during the U.S. War of 1812—the fall of Detroit to the British Canadians. The account in the *College Outline Series* (Krout, 1935) is a somewhat sketchy analysis of the content, evidently intended to help students to pass an objective, short-answer test of factual knowledge:

> THE OFFENSIVE AGAINST CANADA (1812–1815) The first attack against Canada was a failure. Hull surrendered Detroit, Smythe and Van Rensselaer failed at Niagara, Dearborn never crossed the border. (p. 71)

Plainly, this prose corresponds to none of the criteria used to determine aesthetic quality, nor was it intended to have any such value.

In a teacher's edition of a textbook, May (1989) gives another account:

> *Attacking Canada.* The United States planned a three-pronged invasion of Canada, led by Major Henry Dearborn at Lake Champlain, General William Hull at Detroit, and Major General Stephen Van Rensselaer at Niagara. . . . General William Hull surrendered to a much smaller British force without firing a shot. . . . In a court-martial, Hull was sentenced to death for cowardice. . . . But he escaped punishment due to his record in the Revolution. (pp. 321–322)

A set of notes addressed to the teacher accompanies the text:

> OBJECTIVES
> After studying this lesson, students should be able to (1) list reasons why the United States was unprepared for war, (2) realize that the War of 1812 ended in a virtual deadlock, and that the peace treaty solved nothing, (3) know that the Battle of New Orleans was actually fought after the war had ended, (4) recognize that the War of 1812 promoted nationalism in the United States.

READING SKILLS
Supporting details . . . make two lists. . . .
CRITICAL THINKING
Identifying Issues and Motives. . . . Oliver Perry commented that blacks in
his command "seemed absolutely insensible to danger." One reason was surely
the desire for freedom. Develop other reasons. (pp. 321–322)

Considered academically, this account differs from the first because it offers more information and has some narrative elements: the United States
planned the invasion, General Hull surrendered to a much smaller British
force without firing a shot, Hull escaped the death sentence. Notice that
the notes to the teacher do not deal with this passage at all, nor do they
call for any narrative; indeed, they certainly do not deal with the possibility of an aesthetic response to anything connected with the fall of Detroit.
     Bragdon and McCutchen (1981) deal with the event this way:

> The results of this unpreparedness were seen at once. Small but ably led
> Canadian forces took Detroit and two forts on Lake Michigan. An American
> attack across the Niagara River was turned back. No serious attempt was made
> to take Montreal. (p. 210)

This account places the fall of Detroit in a larger context: unpreparedness
for war. The details of the event are ignored. Earlier, we considered the
grandeur of some conceptions of history as an aesthetic quality. Here, the
event is placed in a larger context, unpreparedness, and thereby rises above
the simple facts.
     Compare these texts with Swinton's account, published in 1880:

> A small British force now appeared before Detroit. The American soldiers were
> perfectly confident they could hold the place against the British. Neverthe-
> less, when Hull was called on to surrender, he hung out the white flag and
> capitulated without striking one blow. The army and the whole country were
> very indignant at this disgraceful affair, and Hull's name was struck from the
> rolls of the army. (p. 17)

This is followed by an exercise item at the bottom of the page: "Give an
account of the surrender of Detroit." The selection has more of an aesthetic appeal than the preceding ones; it specifically seeks to arouse the
reader's feelings or recalled emotion. The people are "perfectly confident"
or "indignant," Hull's decision was "disgraceful," and his name was "struck
from the rolls." As historiography, the account is somewhat lacking. As
writing, it has some aesthetic quality.

A 1970 account by Hofstadter, Miller, and Aaron has a strong narrative flow, but it does not seek to involve the reader emotionally. There is no implied judgment of Hull, nor speculation about feelings in the country. This is "objective" military history.

> [T]he United States, at the opening of the war, tried three timid and uncoordinated forays against Canada. . . . The first of these forays, in July 1812, found General William Hull not only failing to penetrate Canada from Detroit, but being forced to yield Detroit to the brilliant Canadian, General Isaac Brock. . . . In 1814, Hull was sentenced to death by a courtmartial . . . but was allowed to escape the penalty because of his record in the Revolution. (p. 349)

This rather dispassionate account contrasts with one published by Hale in 1830:

> The troops, cool and undaunted, awaited in good order the approach of the enemy, anticipating an easy victory. To the astonishment of all, General Hull forbade the artillery to fire, and hung out a white flag in token of a wish to capitulate.
>   It is impossible to describe the indignation of the soldiers and citizens, when they saw themselves delivered, by the authority of one man, into the power of an enemy whom they supposed they might easily have conquered. (p. 149)

This passage is clearly narrative in form. The troops await; they are surrendered against their will; the country is outraged. The style is rhythmic, the phrases have an almost poetic ring:

> The troops
> cool and undaunted
> awaited in good order
> the approach of the enemy
> anticipating
> an easy victory.

The impact, or expression of aesthetic truth, of the passage calls out whatever experience the reader has had with betrayal.

A final example is Graff's (1967) account of the event under the heading "unsatisfactory leadership":

> A third figure of importance who had little to contribute to military success was William Hull, a fifty-nine-year-old hero of the American Revolution. Hull

was persuaded by President Madison to accept a commission as a brigadier general. Madison sent him to take over a force ordered to Detroit.

Disaster at Detroit. Hull was expected to march from Detroit into what is now Ontario and capture the area. The War Department thought that numerous Americans living there would rise up against the British at the first sight of the Stars and Stripes. The American plan for winning the war was summed up in the slogan, "On to Canada!"

Disregarding the British troops and the Indians back of him, Hull set out for Canada on July 12, 1812. As he did so, the British quickly captured Fort Dearborn (on the site of present-day Chicago) and Michilimackinac. The able English general, Isaac Brock, moving westward from Fort Niagara to Detroit, cut Hull off from his base. This gave Hull no choice but to surrender. (pp. 294–295)

The form, style, and content of this passage seem to fit one another well. The form, a narrative, is established at once, when Hull is introduced. It flows to its climax, when he surrenders. The style is almost journalistic: "Hull set out. . . . As he did so. . . ." There is tension (the War Department's error in judgment). The impact of the passage depends on how the reader sees the content; one either identifies with Hull or sees the event as "unsatisfactory leadership."

Aesthetic judgments are, of course, personal. I have arranged the preceding accounts in an order of increasing aesthetic quality, according to my judgment. For me, the 1830 text by Hale and the Graff passage have much more impact, or expressiveness, or aesthetic truth, than do the others.

It is important for students to learn to distinguish serious historical writing from propaganda. Comparisons of the kind illustrated here offer an opportunity to make the distinction. The Hale text has considerable aesthetic appeal, but compared to the Graff, it is propaganda. Propaganda may be seen as biased and incomplete, but well written and full of appeal to one's remembered emotions. Aesthetic truth can be in conflict with factual truth. The point here, however, is that well-written history, which has good aesthetic quality, is likely to have a much greater impact on students than mere factual accounts.

Let us examine these texts aesthetically, in greater detail. The form of the writing differs from one text to another. The Hale text is organized in narrative form. Events begin and come to a climax; one has a sense of people acting. The Swinton text also uses narrative form, but there is no sense of people, only of societies and military units. The *College Outline* account is just that: an outline. The Bragdon and McCutchen text dismisses the event as a minor example of its thesis about unpreparedness. The Hofstadter text is cool and objective. There is no thesis; there are no people; there is only a military event involving two generals, one brilliant, the other disgraced. The Graff text has a much fuller form. The narrative marches forward to its climax with supporting detail and a sense of drama (people are expected to do things; Hull disregards the enemy behind him; Brock is "able"; Hull finally "had no choice"). The May text contrasts with the Graff and the Hale accounts in that it is an example of technical educational writing, with the text pointed not at the reader, not at aesthetic considerations, but at "objectives" that are factual, cool, and test-oriented.

What of the appeal—the calling out of relevant personal experience and sensation—the aesthetic truth? The Hale text appeals to one's sense of betrayal, and the Graff text appeals to one's sense of inept management. The other texts make little or no appeal to one's experience. They are factual, distant, and uninvolving.

Because of their style, their portrayal of people in action, and what they express, the Graff and the Hale versions come closer than the others to leaving the reader with a sense of the goodness of fit, a feeling of consummation that lingers after the text has been put aside. The event has life. People are "able," "disgraced," or "cool"; there is "indignation," "astonishment," and "disaster."

As history, the Hofstadter and the Graff texts are probably the most successful. They are complex and well organized. Each arises from a larger conception of the event; the other texts came nearer to merely reporting it. But other things being equal, the aesthetic quality, or aesthetic truth, of the text will determine its impact on the student-reader.

Mathematics

The aesthetic quality of mathematical statements lies chiefly in the goodness of fit of their components. We have mentioned earlier Einstein's famous statement ($E = mc^2$) of the relationship between energy, mass, and movement, which is elegant because of the perfection of fit among its elements, each of which is highly complex. Logical statements can have the aesthetic appeal of no lost motion, they are parsimonious. The math work of some students will be "messy" in the sense that there is much lost motion in it. Students can be brought to an awareness of the beauty of mathematical formulations if they will consider the "goodness of fit" of the elements in such statements.

Science

Science is full of aesthetic qualities. One need only consider a sunset or sunrise, meaningful sounds, life forms of many kinds, the elegant arrangement of atoms in a molecule, a chemical formula, or the phenomena of growth and change, in order to bring to awareness the aesthetic qualities of existence itself. There are astonishing questions—such as "where did life come from?"—the mere asking of which will have an enlarging effect on the questioner.

Literature

Literature, as one of the arts, has aesthetic truth as its principal quality. This is often overlooked by teachers who ask only that students prove, through a written report, that they have read some masterpiece. It is through the aesthetic analysis of serious literary work that students can be brought to an understanding of its basic value. A recitation of the superficial qualities of a work—plot, characters, technical form, and the rest—is so superficial that school literature, for a great many students, is mere entertainment and often boring. The union of form, content, and style in the best literature, both poetry and prose, both drama and fiction, can be brought to the awareness of students through discussion and analysis and through the reading of responses to the work by the better critics.

The Arts

The Arts are, of course, usually intended to evoke an aesthetic experience. The nature and quality of the experience differ greatly within each of the arts and across all of them. It is easy to find the experience within the recognized masterpieces, whether of ballet, painting, poetry, or the others. As was observed in the case of transcendent experiences, however, the aesthetics of the popular culture also ought to be considered. Great popular composers, such as Duke Ellington, or great dancers, such as Bill Robinson, express considerable aesthetic depth and ought to be included in one's repertoire of taste.

The School Culture

The notion of a school culture has only recently become widely recognized. The school culture, like any culture, consists of the customs, the rules, the reward and punishment system, the symbols, the language, the manner of dress, and, especially, the publicly shared values that characterize it.

All of these have aesthetic meaning. Among adolescents, fads in dress come and go; so do fads in speech. Without denying the inevitability and often the legitimacy of such fads, their aesthetic quality can be brought up for discussion. Some dress fads apparently are statements of adolescent rebellion. How successful they are as statements depends in part on their aesthetic quality—how well do the style, form, and content fit together? A similar question can be raised about the accepted standards for popularity and exclusion, for the settlement of disagreements, for the treatment of teachers and other school officials, and for the basic relationship between the administration of the school and the students. Indeed, because the quality of the school culture depends in large part on its aesthetic quality, it is worth discussing.

Like the other aspects of the self set forth in the Curriculum Matrix, the development of the aesthetic self is complex. Here, we have attempted to describe enough of it to permit a teacher to pursue its complexity throughout the curriculum. The aesthetic quality of the students' experience is always present, determining much of the value they learn to associate with the various aspects of schooling.

We turn now to another of the areas of the self, the physical self. Aesthetic judgment of our physical appearance is commonplace, but there is much more to it than that. Although we don't ignore athletics, we do ignore the body as part of the whole self. Yet it is a fact that all of the attributes of the self discussed in this book occur within the physical self.

CHAPTER 4

The Physical Self

A mature attitude toward the physical self would be autonomous: individuals would reach their own judgments about the meaning of the fact that they are physical beings. People would no longer judge themselves solely through the eyes of others. Girls would no longer judge their appearance by comparing themselves with professional models; boys would no longer assess themselves solely through gang approval, athletic appearance, or any other form of peer judgment.

CURRENT CONCEPTS

Here, we shall explore the concept of the physical self in order to see what teachers can do, within the normal course of class instruction, to help students find enlightenment of the physical aspects of their humanness throughout their school experience.

The first thing to understand about the self is that it functions as a whole. Because all the facets of the self interact, a change in one affects all the others. The body is one of the facets; therefore it is integral to the whole self. In its own way, it is expressive. It penetrates, it even controls, all of one's experience.

This basic understanding is contradicted by the entire tradition of formal schooling. Its ideal is expressed in an ancient formulation: *mens sana in corpore sano* (a sound mind in a sound body). That implies that the mind is one entity, the body another. In fact, the body was once believed to be basically evil; the remains of this attitude were made a permanent part of our culture during the eighteenth century by Descartes who wrote, "*Cogito ergo sum*" (I think, therefore I am). The Cartesian separation of mind from body rules educational thinking to this day.

This tradition has had a destructive effect on children and adolescents that goes beyond the sense of one's physical self. Young children become aware of their selves only gradually and imperfectly. Adolescents, in their rough-and-tumble search for self-definition, very often develop a skewed self-concept. Our cultural tradition offers little help in the difficult journey from childish dependence to adult autonomy. Many an adult remains childishly dependent on others for approval, with (among other things) an undeveloped view of his or her physical self.

These unfortunate beliefs and attitudes show in our ambivalent attitude toward physical education. On the one hand, substantial amounts of education money are spent on space and equipment for physical activity of various kinds, and school sports are given a great deal of attention. On the other hand, accomplishment in sports and physical education is not valued nearly as much as achievement in academic subjects. Most students get the message: physical activity and skill are fun, and they may be rewarded in the short term, but they are not really important. The body is valuable only as a means toward social approval. And of course, one must remain healthy to accomplish the really important things in life.

Those in physical education at the college and university level have responded to this situation. Since 1950, many departments of physical education have sought to emphasize the more fundamental aspects of their field. They have given themselves new names, such as kinesiology or movement science, and have pursued several subspecialties. Corbin (1993, pp. 546–556) warns that too often these developments have led to neglect of what had been the departments' main raison d'être, the professional development of physical educators.

The physical self as a facet of the total self should be sought in the curriculum. The public confusion about this whole matter flies in the face of the fact (established in the West only during the present century) that we are psychosomatic beings, that we function as whole beings, including the body-mind. Methany (1968) describes how movement penetrates consciousness:

> [W]e may note that all man-made forms of consciousness, however they may be perceived, may function as symbols: forms, characteristics, the properties of being, denotation, and connotation. . . . [These movements] also serve to evoke other ideas, feelings, and emotions which are connoted rather than denoted by our recognition of certain patterns within the form. (p. 38–39)

Most of what has been studied about the physical self fails to project a unified person. Such inquiry takes the body to be a separate object, to be studied and understood by itself. Such literature falls into two categories: physical development, or growth; and physical disorders, their avoidance and their cure. More recently, the body has been explored psychologically, and a third category has been added—body image. The findings in all three of these fields—physical development, physical disorders, and body image—have been interesting and instructive, but they do not add up to a realization of the physical self.

Such a realization would include these three areas, but it would incorporate them into a larger sense of self. This larger sense has been with us since the days of William James. As Jersild (1952, p. 65) pointed out, "in speaking of the 'physical self', William James used an apt expression to call attention to the fact that a person's physical features have an important place in his concept of himself."

This larger sense understands the physical self as expressive; it includes body language. It goes beyond physical appearance as a social affair, including the stereotyping that accompanies one's appearance. Some attention is given to this notion in the literature on body image, but that literature deals chiefly with the body as a collection of more or less discrete organs and functions and with their change with growth and development. It deals only incidentally with opinions about the social acceptability of one's personal appearance.

The more recent literature includes broadly determined standards, as distinguished from strictly physical standards. It includes the new emphasis (anticipated by Methany, 1968) on the effect of physical experience on the structuring of one's world. The false division between body and mind is being remedied from two other sources: East Asian thought and recent philosophic writing.

Zen Buddhism does not separate mind from body. Through the practice of meditation, one clears the mind of what are considered extraneous matters (this is very difficult to do) and seeks to achieve a pure sense of existence, a sense of one's wholeness as a human being. Western cultures long evaded, even ridiculed, this approach. However, in recent years it has achieved a certain validity. Even in medicine, where it is called the "relaxation response," meditation has been found to lower blood pressure. A very limited amount of experimentation suggests that meditation does, indeed, produce altered states of consciousness. At present, a few enthusiasts in the West are exploring this aspect of East Asian culture.

Recent philosophic writing has elaborated on the connection between body and mind. Johnson (1987, pp. 125–126) finds that the most primary physical expressions, such as the experiences of force, path, inner and outer, climbing, and many other infantile experiences, become prominent adult metaphors, such as *climbing* the ladder of success, taking the *path* to freedom, and *out* of sorts. Later, they become "image schemata" (e.g., blockage, enablement, iteration, and so forth) determining how one structures one's interaction with all aspects of the environment.

Gallagher (1995, pp. 225–244) distinguishes body image from body schema. *Body image* is an awareness of the body and its functions. *Body schema* operates in a holistic, unified way; it operates before one consciously intends to act; it shapes and controls action. We are, after all, bound by our senses and by what we have learned through interaction with the environment. We apply these learnings, unconsciously, in all parts of our encounters with the world.

In summary, seven aspects of the physical self should be sought out if one intends to find opportunities to increase students' awareness of their physical selves:

1. Physical growth—changes in the body that accompany increasing age
2. Health—prevention of physical disorders
3. Body image—awareness of the bodily organs and functions, awareness of one's appearance
4. Movement, including sports and dance
5. Body language—nonverbal expressiveness
6. Metaphors deriving from primary physical experiences
7. Image schemata, including path, cycle, blockage, and so forth

Literature

One does not expect to find the physical self in Literature, given the way that subject is ordinarily offered. Here we shall look for opportunities to make students aware of it in the literature they read, because students who achieve this awareness will perceive depths in their reading that are now invisible to them. The literature usually assigned in high school classes is generally considered "good." The difference between good literature and mediocre literature is depth: Good literature has enough depth to repay close examination; mediocre literature has only surface value.

By way of example, we shall analyze some exercepts from good literature looking for their expression of the physical self. The aspects of the physical self listed above provide a framework for this analysis.

Physical Development and Health. These two aspects of the physical self did not appear in the literature I examined here, but they are treated extensively in textbooks on physiology and health. In literature, one would look for portrayals of changes in behavior as a consequence of physical development and aging, as when a boy's voice changes or someone's hair becomes gray. Similarly, one would look for the effects of physical impairment or physical well-being on a character's behavior or view of the world.

Body Image. This aspect of the physical self is the actual subject of this selection from Walt Whitman's "I Sing of the Body Electric" in *Leaves of Grass* (1855/1959):

> The expression of a well made man appears not
>   only on his face
> It is in his walk . . . the carriage of his
>   neck . . . the flex of his waist and knees
>   . . . dress does not hide him
> The strong sweet supple quality he has strikes
>   through the cotton and flannel.
> To see him pass conveys as much as the best
>   poem perhaps more,
> You linger to see his back and the back of his
>   neck and shoulderside.

Movement. Early in *Native Son*, Richard Wright (1966) brings forth Bigger, the main character, by the way he moves:

> He stretched his arms above his head and yawned; his eyes moistened. The sharp precision of his world of steel and stone dissolved into blurred waves. He blinked and the world grew hard again, mechanical, distinct. A weaving motion in the sky made him turn his eyes upward; he saw a slender streak of billowing white blooming against the deep blue. (p. 19)

Body Language. Shakespeare's *Macbeth* is a blood-soaked tragedy. Blood appears constantly, literally and figuratively. Pity and terror are evident in almost every line, and they are invoked through the body. The witches, who appear immediately, speak with body language, as seen in Banquo's description of them:

> What are these
> That look not like th' inhabitants o' the
>   earth
> And yet are on't? Live you? Or are you
>   aught
> That man may question? You seem to understand
>   me,
> By each at once her choppy finger laying
> Upon her skinny lips: you should be women,
> And yet your beards forbid me to interpret
> That you are so. (Act I, Scene 5)

Throughout this great tragedy the witches themselves refer to the physical self. Their well-known incantation is intended to be horrifying:

> Nose of Turk and Tartar's lips
> Finger of birth-strangled babe
> Ditch-delivered by a drab
> Make the gruel thick and slab. (Act IV, Scene 1)

Metaphor. In the same play (Act V, Scene 1) Lady Macbeth, sleep-walking, constantly washes her hands. The word *out* reminds us of the metaphor that grows from infantile physical experience: "Out, damned spot! Out, I say!"

Do these excerpts shed any light on Shakespeare and his times? Do they enlarge our personal worlds to include those times? The witches, brides of Satan, speak of physical existence. Macbeth, Lady Macbeth, Malcolm, Banquo, and the others speak in elevated, philosophical terms of their feelings and their actions, except when they are desperate; then their language becomes physical. What did Shakespeare think that his audience believed about the body? Do these verses imply anything to us about ourselves? Perhaps.

Image Schemata. Recall that *image schemata* are transformed metaphors that shape our way of "having a world." Whitman's (1855/1959) "Song of Myself" provides an example:

> I find that I incorporate gneiss and coal and
>   long-threaded moss and fruits and grains
>   and esculant roots
> And am stucco'd with quadrupeds and birds all
>   over, and have distanced what is behind me
>   for good reason,
> And call anything close again when I desire it. (p. 55)

Once we become aware of the physical self, we see it almost everywhere. Here is an example of body image from Gogol's (1925) "The Cloak" (sometimes translated as "The Overcoat"):

> All this, the noise, the talk, and the throng of people, was rather overwhelming to Akaky Akakiyevich. He simply did not know where he stood, or where to put his hands, his feet, and his whole body. Finally he sat down by the players, looked at the cards, gazed at the face of one and another, and after a while began to gape, and to feel that it was wearisome, the more so, as the hour was already long past when he usually went to bed. (p. 63)

Or consider this, from the poem "Physiologus" by Josephine Miles (1983):

> This weight of knowledge dark on the brain is
>   never
> To be burnt out like a fever
> But slowly, with speech to tell the way and
>   ease it,
> Will sink into the blood, and warm, and
>   slowly
> Move to the veins, and murmur, and come at
>   length
> To the tongue's tip and the finger's tip
>   most lowly
> And will belong to the body wholly. (p. 7)

Whether the author is Twain, Scott, Poe, Wordsworth, or someone more contemporary, we will find the physical self operating within the work. Teachers of literature constantly have the opportunity to increase students' awareness of themselves as whole human beings, including their physical selves.

Social Studies/History

Written History is as full of the physical self as is any other form of literature. War, for example, is a physical affair, as well as a political, economic, cultural, social, and even scientific phenomenon. If one asks a returning soldier what it was like, he is likely to first report how it was physically.

In seeking out the physical self in History, we can use the categories discussed earlier: development and growth, health, body image, movement, body language, metaphor, and image schemata. We can examine the age and development of historical personages: how old was Caesar at his peak, or Benjamin Franklin? Did any of the U.S. presidents grow in office? What was the influence of Franklin D. Roosevelt's health on his behavior as president? Do national leaders look different from others, or do they look like everyone else? Why do soldiers march in order? Larger questions can be examined: Why did the Napoleonic invasion of Russia fail? How does field labor affect the politics of a country? What was the effect of the monasteries on European culture? What was it like to live in them?

Mathematics

The most obvious application of Math to the physical self is through measurement: body dimensions (proportion of head to torso, legs to arms, and so forth); movement (how fast, how complex); body temperatures; ratios, such as age to size and gender to height; and vocabulary, for example, the sources of the Math vocabulary (in, out, up, down, balance, equality, strength of ideas, and so forth).

Science

The life sciences are the most obvious places to introduce the physical self. How would the world seem if we were put into the bodies of insects, keeping our present intelligence? How would our sense of the world change if our senses were like those of a dog or a bat? What is the smallest thing Science has found? The largest? What does the passage of time have to do with the span of life? And what about the word *span*?

Vocational and Technical

The large idea in the vocational and technical fields is this: in what way do technical machines extend the bodily senses or other physical functions? Does a computer do anything that the body does not do? Why have computers? What do such office vocations as accounting have to do with the body?

The Arts

The place of the physical self in the Arts has occupied the attention of artists of all kinds since antiquity. Greek sculpture celebrates the body; so does dance. The physical self is slightly less apparent in music, until one remembers that all musical performance is a physical act. Drama does not take place until actors speak and move. And so on. The Arts, all of them, celebrate our physical selves.

In general, the awareness of one's self as a physical being, with as much detail as is now available, is an essential part of the sense of one's existence. There are those who separate mind from body, choosing to emphasize their bodies; some models do that, as do some athletes. Others do it, too, and they pay the penalty that is exacted for overspecialization. The idea is to avoid living an unbalanced existence; we must allow for the unity of body, mind, sensation, and the other properties we share as human beings.

Like the other topics of this book, the treatment of the physical self opens up a highly complex area. If teachers are aware of this aspect of our existence, they may find ways to make their students aware of it as a positive part of themselves, and help rid them of over-dependence on social approval of their physical appearance. We turn now to an examination of the social self in more detail.

CHAPTER 5

The Social Self

One of the more familiar aspects of the self is the social self. Like the other parts of the self we have included among the purposes of education, the social self is highly complex, and its appearance in school subjects amounts to putting one complexity into another. Social development is now one of the more commonly recognized purposes of organized schooling. Students have always had to learn how to behave with their peers, and the classroom is a social situation. Until the twentieth century, however, the social development of children and young people was not a concern of teachers, except as it pertained to keeping order and to penalizing cheating.

THE CONCEPT "SOCIAL"

With the development of child psychology as a field of study and experimentation came the realization that social development was a desirable, even essential, part of organized education. Beginning early in the twentieth century, the various aspects of social growth became more and more central to the attention of teachers and students.

The idea that we are social beings arises from the plain fact that we deal with human relationships constantly. Each of us belongs to many types of communities, such as residential, social, professional or occupational, generational, political, educational, religious, familial, and cultural. Each of these communities has its own structure, its own rules and customs, even its own language and symbol systems. When we relate to others, we modify our personal styles to fit the community we are in. Indeed, some of us modify our social styles so much that we seem to be different persons when we change communities. When we speak of the social self, we mean the relational self. It follows that to study the social self, we must be familiar with social communities, for it is our relationships with members of communities that define us as social beings.

At present, there is no unifying theory of social development. The field consists of several categories of research and speculation, and some application of theories of learning and personality. We shall examine several of these categories here. To illustrate how they may appear in school, we shall show how each of them appears in Science, as well as in other subjects.

Here we consider six of these categories: cooperation and competition; moral development; peer relations; aggression; empathy and sympathy; and similarities and differences. We shall examine how each of them appears in science, as well as in other subjects.

Cooperation and Competition

Cooperation and competition function powerfully in almost any community. Cooperation requires a set of skills and attitudes that are hard to learn, especially for children. A bright 6-year-old I know understands cooperation in a way typical of children: "Cooperation means that you do what the teacher says." That is, you cooperate with the teacher's specification of what you do as a part of a group.

Deutsch (1973) has studied cooperation and encourages it, explaining:

> [Why a] cooperative process is likely to lead to a productive conflict resolution:
> 1. It encourages open and honest communication of relevant information between the participants.
> 2. It encourages the recognition of the legitimacy of the other's interests and of the necessity to search for a solution that is responsive to the needs of each side.
> 3. It leads to a trusting, friendly attitude, which increases sensitivity to similarities and common interests, while minimizing the salience of differences. (p. 56)

The difficulties in learning cooperation arise from the fact that children, like most adults, are pragmatic; they rarely do things just because they ought to. Their behavior is governed for the most part, not by principles, but by consequences. The consequences of cooperation are undramatic, compared with the consequences of other social behaviors. Children find them invisible and therefore hard to value.

Classroom teachers often divide students into groups with a common assignment in order to encourage cooperation. These efforts may succeed, but they often fail because there are many difficulties. One person may dominate the others, whereupon the assignment gets done, but the leader has simply taken the teacher's place and the idea of cooperation is lost. Sometimes the learning experiences are limited to the most articulate member, who does all the work while the others "goof off." Other times the children may compete instead of working together, whereupon the supposedly cooperative project disintegrates into a number of unrelated solo efforts. Some teachers try to help students learn from these difficulties by leading class discussions about such failures. They try to bring out the skills of cooperation: how to plan, how to listen, how to summarize, how to delegate, how to include everyone, how to reach a mutually acceptable goal, and how to resolve disagreements.

Perhaps we should substitute the word, *collaboration* for the term *cooperation*. Collaboration is an active process; cooperation suggests an attitude more than it does a series of actions. If they learn something about how to collaborate and if they have had the experience of cooperation or collaboration brought to their awareness, children may choose it as a course of action inasmuch as it yields desirable results. Only after such experience will children come to view cooperativeness as having intrinsic value.

Competition is another matter. People compete to win something scarce—a market, a score, a prize. There can be only one winner; the others are not winners and they may be losers.

Applied to education, such competition makes no sense, since education is not a scarce object. Thus school grades are substituted for education because high grades can be made artificially scarce. Competition for school grades misrepresents the purpose of schooling; grades are something artificial superimposed on what is actually a life-long process. This artificiality explains the low correlation between school grades and life success.

Competition exists in the adult world, of course. Among scientists, there is competition to be the first to publish a finding. Because prestige, not money, is the principal reward in the university where most scientific research is done and because publication yields prestige, scientists fear that their work will be anticipated. The search for prestige is present throughout the university. Individuals and departments compete for recognition, sometimes by the lay press but always by peers within the various disciplines or fields of action.

In *The Double Helix*, for example, J. D. Watson (1968) describes the competition to be the first to unlock the structure of DNA. Later receiving the Nobel Prize for their work, Watson and his partner, H. C. Crick, struggled to win against the great American chemist, Linus Pauling. Watson and Crick cooperated; they competed against Pauling. The structure of DNA would probably have been found sooner, and with much less stress, if Watson, Crick, Pauling, and other scientists had cooperated. But they were all members of a scientific community that did not reward such cooperation.

The lesson in this for children and young people is that cooperation, with all its complexities and difficulties, often saves time and surely reduces emotional stress. It is so hard to learn, however, that even great individuals sometimes have trouble substituting cooperation for destructive competition.

There are other illustrations of destructive competition in science. Joseph Priestley, the great English chemist of the eighteenth century, refused to acknowledge the discovery of oxygen for 35 years because it replaced his theory about phlogiston. In another example, it was found after his death that Sir Cyril Burt, the English psychologist, had falsified data. Such instances are rare. In science, the rules of the community are well known and strict: always give both sides of the question completely, never ever cheat, and always acknowledge others' work.

Not all competition is destructive, however. It often results in improved products, greater efficiency in manufacture, and better relationships between customers and those who serve them. In academia, competition may keep a researcher at his task longer than would otherwise be the case. History is full of examples of beneficial competition, such as, the competitive voyages of discovery during the fifteenth and sixteenth centuries. Competition has revolutionized communications technology during the late twentieth century. In literature, authors compete for critical attention. Although there are a few lonely originators like James Joyce, the great majority of authors learn from each other. The same thing can be said of the graphic and the performing arts.

It is essential that students learn about the relationship between cooperation and competition and that they become articulate about the skills involved in each. In science, students might form small groups and compete to answer a question like "What really happens when a liquid is 'sucked' into a container?" The students would learn something about teamwork, or cooperation, as well as competition, especially if these dynamics were brought to their attention. Other questions can be raised in other subject areas: Why do pollsters report probable error? Why does the weatherman limit his TV predictions to five days? What is the difference, if any, between a poem and a jingle?

Moral Development

Morality is the knowledge of the difference between right and wrong, and the ensuing rules and customs, in human conduct. As Piaget (1965, p. 13) says, morality develops from heteronomy to autonomy, that is, from the dependent rule following of infants and young children to the independent conduct of adults. Adults are aware of society's rules, but their conduct is based essentially on their own rules, the principles that make up their own knowledge of right and wrong—their consciences.

Questions arise: Whose rules are being followed? What are the rules? Why? Moral development may be said to be the answers to these questions achieved by people as they grow up.

Little children do not seek to understand the rules given them by adults; they simply accept them. However, Piaget reminds us that children make their own rules when they are free from adults, as his Geneva children did when they played games of marbles.

For adults, moral behavior is fair and just behavior among people, at least according to almost all research on the subject. The possibility that moral behavior might also be directed inward, toward one's self, seems not to have been investigated. Kohlberg (1984, p. xv) quotes Plato, Dewey, and Piaget as asserting that "justice [is] the first virtue of a person because it is the first virtue of society."

Kohlberg (1984, pp. 624–631) sees moral development as proceeding through three large stages, each divided into two parts (resulting in stages 1 and 2, 3 and 4, 5 and 6), as follows:

1. *Heteronomous Morality:* defining "what makes something wrong . . . by authority rather than by cooperation among people"
2. *Pragmatism:* maximizing the satisfaction of one's needs and desires while minimizing negative consequences
3. *Interpersonally Normative Morality:* trusting relationships among people, embodied in a set of shared norms
4. *Social System Morality:* a set of codes that apply impartially to all members
5. *Human Rights and Social Welfare:* an examination of actual laws and rules to see whether they preserve fundamental human rights and values; a society-creating, rather than a society-maintaining, perspective
6. *Principles Internalized:* a self-conscious structure for moral decision making, which becomes part of one's self

Because people develop unevenly—remaining like children in some ways, achieving adulthood in others—the various aspects of moral development develop unevenly and irregularly. A person may act like an adult in some ways, like a little child in others, like an adolescent in still others.

The moral codes of the various disciplines offered in school are equally uneven. In the scientific community, for example, the moral code is largely quite adult, but in some ways less so. Hagstrom (1965, pp. 9–10) points out that the values of the scientific community are ingrained in the training of students. "[T]he teacher's evaluation tends to be taken by the student as an indication of what he 'is.'" If what he "is" is defined by someone else, he is in Kohlberg's stage 4. Like the adolescent, his self-definition, hence his self-esteem, is in the hands of others; he is other-directed. The same thing is true in some degree for members of the other academic communities—historians, mathematicians, even literary scholars and analysts.

It seems likely that class discussion of moral development would be fruitful if it dealt with questions such as the following: In what degree have I defined myself morally, or have I left the defining of my moral self to others? Whose rules do I follow? Is it ever okay to break an existing rule?

Peer Relations

In many communities, including classroom communities, there is a hierarchy of reputations. Prestige is not evenly distributed. People do not behave privately and publicly in the same ways. The scientific community requires its members to be publicly cordial and respectful toward each other, and even to defend one another against ignorant attack. Privately, particularly concerning technical and scholarly matters, they may be harsh or even cruel.

Among children and young people, the situation is often similar. In their culture, criticism of another's school work is unusual, but criticism of others' social behavior is common. Also, children are often polite and formal with strange children; among their close acquaintances, however, things are different.

"Caring" is one of the few new ideas that have been discussed recently. Nel Noddings (1992, 1995), who has written extensively on this theme, indicates not only how the caring attitude is communicated and the effects of such communication, but how the attitude may be constructed within people and the many forms it takes.

"Playing fair" and "taking turns" come early in children's growth, as kindergarten teachers know well. Awareness of physical and social differences comes during middle childhood, as does the concept of reputation. Adolescence is a period of anxious self-definition, in which peer reputations become so dominant that young people tend to become other-directed, like Hagstrom's (1965) young scientists.

The whole matter of social development deserves direct attention by young people. Discussions of the distinction between private and public behavior, personal and professional relations, the sources and force of reputations, and the nature of positive human relations, all can be brought to the awareness of students, and such discussions are valuable. Opportunities can be found within subject matter as well as within the dynamics of group activity of all kinds. In literature, fiction can be examined for all of these social dynamics; in math, attitudes can be measured and relationships considered; in social studies, the content and techniques of propaganda will repay consideration. Such awareness helps children and young people toward social maturity.

Aggression

Aggression takes many different forms. It often is physical among the young; verbal aggression among adults ranges from the crude to the sophisticated. Both young and old find knowledge of the vocabulary of aggression useful. Name-calling among adults, for example, takes many forms. If one knows the forms, one can deal with name-calling either by avoiding it or by calling attention to it. One of the subtleties of name-calling, in education, is categorizing students into stereotypic groups, such as sub-cultures, talents, ability groups, gender, and sometimes even race.

Among some adults, the form that aggression takes regresses. As aggression moves toward failure, adult behavior may assume more childish forms—name-calling, insults, and even physical attack. Among more mature adults, aggression is replaced by compromise and appeals for justice.

Watson (1968) the scientist had to deal with harsh criticism from his peers at Cambridge. At first, he took the criticism personally, as an attack on his competence. Later, he realized that the criticism had saved him from some fruitless work. Can students learn from Watson's behavior? They can, if the question is raised. How can one deal with harsh criticism, even if it is impersonal? Through childish reciprocity, or getting even? Can one stay above the battle? What does a reasonable response to harsh criticism include? Discussion of such questions might well help some children and young people to avoid reacting blindly.

Can opportunities for discussion of aggression be found in the course of working with subject matter? In Social Studies, there are many opportunities, both in current events and in historic tensions. In Literature, much worthwhile fiction has to do with tension and aggression. The Mathematics community, like the Science community, is dignified, but firm. Perhaps older students might examine Math journals to see how criticism is expressed and countered. There is a vocabulary of aggression, which would repay development and examination with students.

Empathy and Sympathy

The basic expression of empathy is "I know how you feel," a comment that is widely considered to be the most mature of social expressions. This is true only in a limited sense, because individuals differ and feelings, or emotions, are highly complex and personal. What one can know, and communicate, is a general awareness of another's feelings. Usually, it is negative feelings one is in some sense responding to.

Sympathy, on the other hand, involves sharing the feelings of others. The sympathetic response is similar to the feelings of another person. One shares the sadness or the joy. Sympathy is a far more common phenomenon than empathy.

Feelings of empathy or sympathy are ordinarily personal, as between two individuals. They do not ordinarily occur in scholarly communities, as among historians, scientists, or authors. Public communities, such as those defined by race or ethnicity, sometimes contain empathetic or sympathetic customs. Many of us share the feelings of the downtrodden or the unfortunate. As groups, we sometimes share feelings of triumph or its opposites.

The members of scholarly communities do not usually exhibit such feelings toward one another. In their work, scholars are ordinarily cool and logical, or objective. This leads the public to see the members of such communities as impersonal people. As individuals, they are as human as anyone else, of course, and they have all the personal feelings that are common among us. The distinction is between personal and professional behavior.

Children and young people need to learn that distinction. It is one thing to identify with someone's professional work, and another to identify with the human process or the person who produced it. Both are legitimate, but they must not be confused with each other. Empathy and sympathy have to do with the person, not the results. Students who have internalized this distinction have moved toward adulthood.

In classroom work, students ought to learn not only about the disciplined knowledge represented by academic school subjects, but also about the human beings who produced it. Biographies of such people can help young people toward maturity.

Similarities and Differences

The physical similarities and differences among people, as well as their cultural differences in speech or manner, are lost in the work of the scholars whose products we study. Who cares about the culture, or race, or personal manner, of the great figures in our intellectual past? Such matters are interesting, and biographies of these people are written, but our interest in them arises from their achievements and discoveries, not from their personal lives.

The problems that arise from the fact that people are diverse have afflicted our societies since the beginning of time. What the young need to learn is that there are important, and unimportant, similarities and differences among people. Can this be learned as students encounter school subjects?

Certainly it can in the social studies, inasmuch as the understanding of cultures and political systems is central to that field. Literature, too, offers the opportunity to broaden the world of students to include awareness of how people are the same and how they differ, and how these similarities and differences may be understood. It is the wholeness of people, not a stereotypic part of them, that we hope students will understand. Can this be done in Mathematics and the Sciences? It can, through biography, as was pointed out above. It can be done, also, if the substance of Math and Science can be seen as a part of the wholeness of human beings—as a part of the basic human condition, despite other differences.

The school subjects first of all can be seen as human endeavors. Such understandings are a crucial part of the social self. In the degree that they are grasped, social relationships will be healthy, and productive, and mature.

We turn now to the emotional self. Like social development, the emotional development of children and young people has come to be recognized as an essential part of the self during the present century. Also like the social self, the emotional self is a complex, perhaps even a confused, area. We shall examine the nature of the emotional self, as well as our conflicting views of it, as we consider how emotional maturity may be fostered within the usual school subjects.

CHAPTER 6

The Emotional Self

Like other aspects of the human self, the emotional self develops within us. All of us are emotional beings. Someone completely without emotion would be psychotic. In education, however, the emotions have been the object of suspicion, even scorn, since Plato. In the eighteenth century, Samuel Johnson (in his dictionary) defined passion as "a disturbance of the reason." To this day, we educators imply a persona that is unemotional, completely rational at all times, cool, even cold—one with so much self-control that no emotion is ever evident. We seek only to control the emotions, when clearly we ought to acknowledge them as an essential part of their being. We are so taken with the dangers associated with the negative emotions that we ignore the positive ones. Consequently, growing young people seeking emotional maturity, along with the other aspects of maturity, are left to fend for themselves. Teachers and other adults in their lives provide little or no help, and no conscious modeling.

Likewise, psychologists provide little help. Jersild and Holmes (1935, p. 341) pointed out generations ago that there is no certain way to help children avoid emotional problems, and that emotional maturity involves the expression of emotions in socially acceptable ways. More recent psychologists take similar positions.

Nevertheless, we shall examine here the possibility that students' emotional maturity can be enhanced by what teachers do in school. After considering some of what is known about this complex aspect of the self, we shall look for possibilities for emotional awareness within the social studies (presumably, an unlikely area for such a search) and also in other subject areas.

THE NATURE OF EMOTIONS

Any emotion is a complex affair. Although emotions can be specified by name, any actual emotion exists in a context unique to the individual. Joy for one person can be sorrow for another; shame for one can be a source of pride for another. Izard (1991, p. 14) offers a useful definition: "An emotion is experienced as a feeling that motivates, organizes, and guides perceptions, thoughts, and actions."

From this viewpoint, it seems important for growing young people to become aware of their feelings, lest they continue to act toward them like little children, who react to feelings without anything but the most primitive understanding of them. They are inarticulate and unaware, like the boy who explained that he had killed another child "because I was mad." Indeed he was, in the literal sense—he had lost his mind. But his other limitation was that he could not discriminate among his feelings; he blindly reacted to them. Had he been able to discriminate, he might have been able to express the subtle distinctions between irritation, annoyance, anger, outrage, and rage. If he had, perhaps the quarrel would not have spiraled up into a killing.

We shall take the position here that emotional maturity consists in large part of being aware of one's feelings in some detail. Such awareness, in turn, consists in part of being able to give such feelings an accurate name. If you can say it, you are aware of it. Psychiatrists point out that much therapy consists of making people aware of the nature and sources of their feelings. One aspect of this is verbal—the ability to name one's feelings. Once this is accomplished, people can be enabled to respond to them appropriately.

Teachers are not psychiatrists, and we do not intend to meddle with therapy. But we can develop with students a vocabulary of emotion, which is one step along the way to emotional maturity. As it happens, this was the object of literary scholarship before the psychologists began to work on it. Miles (1942/1965) found that Wordsworth had named emotions extensively, thus defying his eighteenth century rationalist upbringing and contributing to the English Romantic movement. "The Idiot Boy" is a good example, but the work is perhaps best summarized in "Lines Composed a Few Miles Above Tintern Abbey," when he recalled the feelings of youth:

> . . . sensations sweet
> Felt in the blood, and felt along the heart.

He continues with the feelings of maturity

> . . . in after years
> When these wild ecstasies shall be matured
> Into a sober pleasure.

In 1969, Joel Davitz published a study of the actual language people use (e.g., "I'm all choked up," "I feel like smiling," "I feel wide-awake") and discovered a number of words that he included in his "Dictionary of Emotional Meaning." He explains:

> I set out to complete a dictionary of common emotional terms that might be of some use in clarifying communication about emotional phenomena. Not by legislating definition but by describing the commonalties of meaning shared by members of a given language community. (p. 3)

Davitz lists the following emotional terms:

admission	determination	gratitude	passion
affection	disgust	grief	pity
amusement	dislike	guilt	pride
anger	elation	happiness	relief
anxiety	embarrassment	hate	remorse
awe	excitement	hope	reverence
boredom	faith	inspiration	sadness
cheerfulness	fear	irritation	serenity
contempt	friendliness	jealousy	shame
contentment	frustration	love	solemnity
delight	gaiety	nervousness	surprise
depression			

Izard (1991, pp. 85–92) distinguishes between "core" definitions such as those by Davitz and what he calls "connotative" meanings. From his point of view, any actual emotion exists in a sort of "cloud" of meaning. For example, interest and excitement go together. Anxiety may well be a combination of distress, anger, shame, shyness, and guilt. He collapses the large number of shades of feeling into several fundamental emotions:

interest–excitement	disgust–revulsion
enjoyment–joy	contempt–scorn
surprise–startle	fear–terror
distress–anguish	shame–shyness–humiliation
anger–rage	guilt

The last two, shame and guilt, are so close together that they may be considered a single fundamental emotion.

Although Izard does not say so, each of these fundamental emotions may be considered as a range. As already pointed out, anger extends from irritation to rage; guilt is at one end of a range that begins with embarrassment. The psychological literature appears not to consider these ranges, but teachers may well find them useful.

Teachers could use the Davitz and Izard lists in discussions with students, seeking to make them aware of the vocabulary of emotions and of the various ranges. With such awareness comes a degree of emotional maturity. Opportunities for such discussions can be found in the course of teaching regular school subjects.

The Social Studies/History

The extensive discussion of the purpose, substance, and practice of the Social Studies is summarized well by Thornton (1994) and will be passed over here in favor of a look within the field for opportunities to enhance students' emotional maturity.

Jenness (1990, p. 24) sets forth the usual school offering in the Social Studies: American History in grades 5, 8, and 11; Geography in grade 7; World History and Cultures in grades 9 and 10; American Government, Civics, and Political Science in grade 12. Sociology and Economics are rarely offered. There is considerable variation in the offering from one state, or even one school district, to another, especially at the early elementary level. However, beginning at grade 4, where state history is often offered, there is a considerable similarity. The most common offering is in History—of the state, of the United States, of the world (chiefly Europe). Current events is also a frequent offering.

Because of their prevalence, history and current events are the most inviting places to seek opportunities to deal with emotion. To find emotion in history, we must first revise our usual approach, which deals only with dates, events, and personages. Instead, raise questions about feelings, like these: How did people feel about these events and personages? How did the personages probably feel? Would their feelings have any influence on events? Role-playing is one way to portray feeling, in addition to the dynamics operating as events unfold.

Another approach can be found in primary documents. To discover what emotions probably entered into the Dred Scott decision, read the decision itself and imagine the contesting arguments and their feelings. At the same time, consider the American system of justice and see how decisions seek to resolve contesting feelings, as well as the conflicting interests.

Dale Brubaker (1963, p. 82) tells of a class considering the debate that preceded the Mexican War of 1845. The class looked at Polk's War Message to Congress and at the Summer Resolution opposing the war with Mexico, both documents being charged with emotion. Brubaker (p. 183) also tells of a class examining the debates that led up to the Civil War. They heard a recording (made by an actor) of the speech by Senator Toombs of Georgia, in which he set forth the Southern position. His presentation was based not only on emotion, but on the Dred Scott decision and on an interpretation of the Constitution.

Several other possibilities exist. Students could role-play the opposing arguments and feelings associated with great events in history. They could write fiction depicting the victims of an unjust society, as Harriet Beecher Stowe did. They could write and deliver propagandistic speeches on opposite sides of historic issues, such as the income tax, or the environment laws. Primary documents can be found in the back files of newspapers, and sometimes in the students' own attics.

The popular media—television, Internet, radio, newspapers, and magazines—all deal with what is sensational and titillating, in search of an audience. As homework, students could be asked to examine the media for statements of feeling associated with events of general interest, as well as with athletic events. Students can be asked to write their own versions of such events. Current events, as well as historical situations, are an unending source of possibilities. How might Boss Tweed, or Boss Daley, or Boss Pendergast have appealed to the emotions? What about the expression of feeling during the Great Depression or World War II? Since people learn what they make, asking students to make emotional statements is a way of helping them to learn the vocabulary of emotion.

The plea here is that, in addition to the intellectual analyses of historical events and personages, students confront directly the emotional content associated with them. The events leading up to the Vietnam War and the War of 1812 can be compared, and the feelings associated with them examined. The possibilities seem endless.

Zevin (1992) sees three dimensions in the social studies: the didactic, the reflective, and the affective. Concerning the affective dimension, he makes direct suggestions:

> in affective roles, you act to bring values, feelings, and sensitive issues to the forefront of discussion. This should be done in a way that helps students to look at themselves and their own behavior as well as [those] of others. (p. 4)

Boutwell (1972) puts the affective curriculum at the heart of the social studies:

> The purpose of social studies within the affective curriculum, then, is to help children become more flexible and adaptable, gain a greater range of insights into the human condition, and thereby gain greater understanding of their own selves. Social studies, in other words, can expand a child's affective repertoire. (p. 184)

This is exactly the point of the present chapter.

In England, Lawton and Dufour (1976) put the matter of values with caution:

> We cannot avoid values. We must still decide, however, the limits to which we, as teachers, have a right to go in the matter of approaching values . . . there are certain substantive values . . . which the school has a duty to transmit. (pp. 34–35)

The Association of Teachers of Social Studies in the City of New York (1977, p. 7) list verbs that "combine the affective and cognitive domains": *express, debate, evaluate, judge, interpret, contract.* Each of these words suggests a classroom activity, especially discussion.

Geography is usually thought of as a factual field and nothing more, until one considers it the way geographers do—as dealing with how people should make use of the earth's surface. For example, the Florida Everglades are said to be dying, and it is proposed that money be raised through taxes to improve matters. Is that fair? To whom? The giant redwood trees of northern California, thousands of years old, are being harvested, never to be replaced. Same questions. The Brazilian forest is being decimated. What is fair? How do people feel about the alternatives? These questions, and others like them, can be raised about many of the issues concerned with the earth's surface.

The other aspects of the Social Studies—economics, political science, social psychology, and the rest—are all studies of the human condition, and are therefore inviting fields for consideration of human emotion. We live in a time of increased urbanization; small rural towns are withering away, together with the family farm. What feelings are associated with this great shift? What changes in values? The United States exists between two other countries, Canada and Mexico. The Canadian culture is quite similar to ours; the Mexican culture is quite different. How do people feel about those facts? How do they feel about our nation's increasing cultural diversity? The social studies offer a place and a time to explore the sensitive matter of human relations in a diverse population, inasmuch as the school population itself is diverse.

Literature

The literature usually offered in school is full of emotion, though this fact is often overlooked. Inasmuch as we are searching for the vocabulary that describes the ranges of the various fundamental emotions, such a search is one kind of worthwhile analysis students might undertake. This is obviously the case in lyric poetry; it is often overlooked in prose fiction and drama. Propaganda is a form of literature; an analysis of the emotional appeals in propaganda would repay the effort.

Mathematics

The most obvious application of Math to emotions is through measurement. How intense, on a numerical scale, is the statement of an emotion? On a scale that runs from apathy to intense feeling, what are the feelings of class members abut referents such as bullying, gifts, bragging, accomplishment, status, school achievement, and popularity?

Science

In the life sciences, particularly, there are opportunities to explore emotions. What are the physical signs of feeling? Answers would include tears, laughter, movement. How do animals express their emotions? Do we express ours in similar ways? What is the difference in this area between humans and animals? Answers might be that humans are far more subtle or that the range of emotions among humans appears to be far greater.

The Arts

The Arts seek to give our emotions direct expression. One might ask students to portray the various emotions in the art forms. One can imagine a class portraying joy, for example, in music, dance, sculpture, and drama. Such an exercise would surely deepen students' awareness of the emotion, and developing such awareness is a primary purpose.

In this chapter, we have explored the emotional self that is part of all of us. In order for children and young people to mature emotionally, they require (among other things) a vocabulary of emotions that permits them to express shades of feeling. In the degree that they can do this, they will become increasingly subtle and sensitive adults. When we succeed in helping students toward emotional maturity, we help them to bring about an essential part of their self-realization.

We next turn from emotional development to what for teachers is the most familiar aspect of the self, intellectual development. Since the field is so familiar and so complex, we shall confine ourselves to only one part, problem solving. In the degree that students grasp this process, their educational progress will be enhanced. Like the preceding chapters in this book, this one seeks only to sketch how this aspect of the self can be found in the curriculum offering, including the unlikely parts.

It is worth emphasizing once more that we deal here with an array of highly complex topics and subjects, which interact endlessly, and which are considered together here only because they coexist in every teacher's classroom.

CHAPTER 7

The Intellectual Self

To teachers, intellectual development is the most familiar of the aspects of the self. It has been studied more than any of the others, and intellectual behavior is what is most often evaluated and reported by schools. Here, we will view it as just one of the several aspects of the self already discussed, every one essential, and each to be found in the usual curriculum offerings.

THE INTELLECTUAL EXPERIENCE

What is meant by *intellect*? Those who have studied it include memory, insight, recognition, knowledge, aptitudes, and what a friend of mine called "minding," or reasoning, or problem solving. Primarily interested in the development of abilities, teachers have always focused on the ability to act intellectually—to solve problems.

Given all this, it is interesting to find that, upon examination, the concept of intellectuality is shot through with ambiguity. As Pole (1975, p. 8) asks, "What, exactly, do we mean by 'equal,' 'fact,' 'belief'?" The answer, it develops, is, "it all depends." And what it depends on is the context. "Things equal to the same thing are equal to each other," we say. What "things"—Automobiles, planets, people, numbers? What does "equal" mean in that statement? It turns out that we are comparing only numbers, a pure abstraction. Only numbers are equal enough to satisfy the statement. We abstract and quantify from reality in order to make such statements.

The language of reasoning, according to Pole (1975, p. 1), is best understood as a set of conventions, and the end of a chain of reasoning, as a judgment, not a conclusion. Reasoning, he suggests, is best thought of as an explanation, "which is bound to start somewhere, with something itself unexplainable." So much for axiomatic truth!

One must begin, therefore, with the understanding that reasoning, or problem solving, is subject to ambiguity and that it seeks sound judgments, not demonstrated conclusions. So viewed, problem solving certainly is

67

characteristic of all kinds of human activity, from the Arts, to the establishing of societies, to the Sciences. Only in abstract Mathematics is it possible to reason without ambiguity. "Pure" reasoning does not exist in the actual world, the world we humans inhabit. We seek to help our students make the best judgments possible, given the ambiguity of the actual world. Any more pretentious objective would be, not reasonable, but dogmatic.

That is why we shall refer here to problem solving, not reasoning, as the most central of the intellectual behaviors. Problems are ordinarily ambiguous, as we shall see, and the judgments reached about them are not perfect, but the best we can manage.

PROBLEM SOLVING

Dewey (1933) equates his "reflective thinking" with problem solving:

> [I]f we are willing to extend the meaning of the word *problem* to whatever—no matter how slight and commonplace in character—perplexes and challenges the mind so that it makes belief at all uncertain, there is a genuine problem, or question, involved. (p. 12)

For Dewey, solving problems, or reflective thinking, involves not only method, but also attitudes, interest, and application. He also suggests that the artist's approach might serve as an ideal to be attained ultimately:

> The familiar fact that creative work in the arts, writing, painting, music, etc., is largely unconscious as to the motives and attitudes of the artist, his mind being fixed on the objects he is dealing with or constructing, suggests the adoption of a like course in both studying and teaching. The artist should be taken as a model rather than the activities of one painfully conscious at every step of just how he is operating. (p. 283)

Dewey (1933, p. 287) sees problem solving wherever he looks. He emphasizes this by pointing again to the arts: "That art originated in play is a common saying. Whether or not the saying is historically correct, it suggests a harmony of mental playfulness and seriousness that describes the artistic ideal."

More recently, thinking about problem solving in the classroom has been influenced by Bloom's (1954) taxonomy and Piaget's (1954) stage theory. Both have been misapplied to curriculum making; neither offers a problem-solving procedure (practice) or proposes a curriculum content (substance). Piaget sought to describe a crucial aspect of child development, and Bloom and his colleagues sought to describe the components of evaluation instruments.

Problems range in structural complexity from "2 + 2 = ?" to "shall we get married?" As we have noted, the actual problems people face are usually messy. Problem solving has come to be viewed by many as on a continuum from well-structured through moderately structured to loosely structured problems. As Kahney (1993) puts it:

> Well structured problems are those for which the initial state, goal state, and legal operators and operator restrictions are all given at the start of the problem. An ill-structured problem is one in which information about either the initial or goal state, or the operators and operator restrictions is incomplete and has to be supplied by the problem-solver. (p. 93)

By "operators" Kahney means the rules or the restrictions to be observed. The structure or principles of a given field would act as operators.

The more tightly structured a problem is, the more specific it is to a particular situation. The judgment made at the end of a sequence is ordinarily specific to the situation. In school, though, we constantly deal with moderately to loosely structured problems and seek generalizations, or principles, rather than specific solutions. For example, the solution to a problem in plane geometry is seen as an illustration of the generalization stated as its premise, or axiom. The same thing is true of problems in chemistry and essays in writing classes—for example, "in this instance, the acid released its hydrogen, as acids always will in these circumstances." Or "this is a well-written essay because it shares certain characteristics of well-written essays." In school, we constantly seek useful generalizations because they are the path toward autonomous maturity.

Several formulas for the teaching of problem solving have appeared during recent years. In one of these Woods (1987) enumerates necessary skills:

> The skills needed in this process include a knowledge base pertinent to the content of the problem, the ability to identify, locate, obtain, and evaluate missing information, the ability to learn on one's own, such thinking skills as analysis (classify, check for consistency, reason, and identify relationships), creative ability to generalize and so simplify and broaden perspectives, such attitudes as motivation and perseverance, ability to cope with ambiguity, fear, anxiety and procrastination, interpersonal and group skills, communication skills, and an awareness of how one thinks, one's personal preference or style when hearing or processing information. In addition, we use an organized approach (or a strategy). (p. 55)

Given this large number of skills, problem solving seems a formidable affair. Very few adults, let alone children and young people, possess all of them. But problems exist and must be solved.

In another formula for the teaching of problem solving, Jonassen (1997, pp. 26–31) suggests a six-step teaching process:

1. *Articulate problem content.* What is the nature of the domain? What constants are imposed by the content? What kinds of problems are solved in this domain? What contextual constraints affect problems?
2. *Introduce problem constraints.* These are often the practical constraints of time and budget, plus such others as peer attitudes and customs and availability of materials.
3. *Locate, select, and develop cases for learners.* Develop cases that represent probable real-world problems in the domain: that is, they are authentic. The obvious source of these cases is interviewing practitioners.
4. *Support knowledge base construction.* Identify the alternative opinions and perspectives with a knowledge base of stories, accounts, evidence, and information that pertain to the problem being considered.
5. *Support argument construction.* Different conceptualizations of the problem lead to different assumptions and the consequent arguments. Learners should be able to articulate these arguments. Prompt with questions such as: Can you ever know for sure that your position is correct? How did you come to hold that point of view? What did you base it on? What does it mean to you if you find that the experts disagree with your idea?
6. *Assess problem solutions.* Was the problem solved—did it go away? Was it solved within the constraints identified earlier? Can the learner explain why and how the problem was solved?

All of the material presented so far will be used to make problem solving a practical object of instruction. All of our sources indicate that knowledge, or information, is required: facts, names, special language or symbols, existing experiences, the structure of the field, often its history. Bloom's "synthesis" (which can be thought of as concept formation) is essential; the information must be put together in such a way as to make the problem solvable (1954, p.162). Evaluation, which can be stated as the goal of the process (i.e., the solution of the problem), is also essential. Finally, we shall borrow the notion of a continuum of problem-solving structures, from ill-structured to well-structured. The solution to ill-structured problems consists of analyzing them into their well-structured subparts and solving these, thus making the overall problem solvable.

From what has been summarized above, we can derive the following seven questions which can be used by teachers as a framework, or guide, for bringing about problem solving.

1. What is the problem? (State it as well as you can.)
2. What practical constraints must be considered?
3. What kind of problem is it? (What is its field, its domain, or its context?)
4. What information, or knowledge, is required?
5. How shall the problem be restated?
6. How shall the solution to the problem be organized? (Are there intermediate goals?)
7. How will you know that the problem has been solved?

These seven questions will be used as a framework to find problem solving in the usual school subjects. Remember, this is only a partial illustration, inasmuch as both intellectuality and each of the school subjects are highly complex. Mathematics will not be included in the discussion that follows because problems in Math are usually well-structured; the goal is clear, and so are the steps required to reach it.

What Is the Problem? State It as Well as You Can.

This question will be considered as it appears in several school subjects. It is necessary to begin here because children's concepts of the problems they face are usually more vague than they could be. The direction, "State it as well as you can," invites them to begin the process of problem identification, which is central to solving the problem.

The Arts. We will begin with the Arts, because they are not usually associated with problem solving. We shall assume that we are working with a middle-grade elementary school class.

Consider first the attitude we shall bring to the task. We have been conditioned to believe that intellectual behavior is entirely a matter of verbal and mathematical skill. Because the arts do not use these symbol systems in a linear, logical way, it can be inferred that the arts are not intellectual.

This belief has created much confusion. Teachers of the mid-twentieth century became convinced that the Arts serve only one purpose: to give expression to deeply placed emotional and developmental states. This belief was urged by people as eminent as Viktor Lowenfeld and various psychoanalysts after Freud. It fit well with the educational climate of those times, during which teachers were urged to make schooling a pleasant, even a joyous, experience and to escape from the artificial, dreary nineteenth century classroom. The Arts, especially, came to be viewed as a safety valve for the release of tensions created by the more formal, presumably more intellectually demanding, parts of the school offering.

This view has led those elementary school teachers who are untrained in the Arts (and that is almost all of them) to believe that their function in the arts is to keep order and get out of the way, lest they interfere with the expressiveness of the children. Indeed, as Barkan (1955) pointed out, some teachers evaluate their work by the number of different media the children employ, thus making it likely that the children will not learn much about any of them. Francisco (1958) was even more explicit:

> Some purists in art education may claim to believe in growth and development through art, but would accomplish the task by eliminating all restraints, all suggestions, and even guidance. The fallacy inherent in the laissez-faire school of thought is that it is unrealistic. (p. 11)

Eisner (1976, p. 9) joined in abandoning the idea that art expression comes purely from within. He pointed out that "[a]t school age nine and ten . . . [children] want to express a more comprehensive . . . repertoire of skills that will enable them to create more visually convincing pictures." Indeed, the essentially untutored development of children's drawings has been documented repeatedly and is familiar to teachers, from the early drawing of a human figure with the arms coming from the head to a picture of a house with a slanted chimney, to a house with many windows and a lollipop tree standing in front.

More recently, Rush (1996) concludes a challenging essay thus:

> Art is language that conveys meaning. When classroom art is problem solving, students develop the capability to be artistically expressive. Students capable of artistic expression transcend the boundaries of self-expression into the broader creative realm of the arts. (p. 52)

The growth of intelligence depends on experience, as Dewey pointed out long ago. If the experience is untutored, intelligence remains uninformed. Actual artists develop what Eisner (1972, pp. 109–110) called "qualitative thought." "As a process of using qualitative thought to solve qualitative problems, such a process can be conceived of as depending on the exercise of qualitative intelligence." It is the development of Eisner's "qualitative intelligence" that we seek to explore here in the arts.

Assume that the class has accepted the assignment, "make a picture of a house." The teacher might now ask for statements of the problem. Students will give a variety of responses, which may lead to a class discussion of the problem. The teacher's purpose at this point is to start the children thinking about their drawings before starting to make them. It has been found that actual artists, when they were children, planned their work. Others simply began it.

Social Studies/History. The children are likely to have been studying American History (see Chap. 3). What is the problem? Following class discussion, possibly they will select the Korean War. The teacher asks, "In what way is that a problem?" The class decides that the problem is, "How did the United States get involved in it?"

The teacher might also lead the class to get beyond political history to some form of social history—perhaps the rise of the Labor movement during the late-nineteenth century. Now, the problem becomes, "Why did the Labor movement begin at that time?"

Literature. At grade 5, the children have encountered some poetry and prose fiction. A class discussion has led them to name as a problem, "Why read fiction?" The teacher will lead the discussion in the direction of increasingly specific answers to that question.

Science. Assume that the class is studying a form of life science—the nature of plant life. The class discussion might lead to a question like, "Why do some plants flourish, and others die, in a garden?" The teacher might lead the students to make the question as specific as possible.

What Practical Constraints Must be Considered?

The practical constraints are introduced at this point in order to give the children a bit of time to think over and digest the discussion that located the problem and made it specific. Most of the constraints are those of common sense: time, materials and equipment, possibly budget. Some constraints arise from the context of the problem; one cannot apply the methods of Science to the Arts, for example. The problem will have to be dealt with within these constraints, but the constraints themselves ought to be discussed: "How much time do we want to give this? What materials will we need? Where are they? Do we need any money to do this? Where shall we get it? How confident are we that we can solve the problem? Do methods exist to solve the problem or must we invent a method?"

What Kind of Problem Is This? What Is its Field, Its Domain?

The responses to this question will differ from one field to another; each has its own structure. As Dewey pointed out, the work of an artist might serve well as a model, so we will begin with the Arts.

The Arts. Once the children have thought about drawing a house, the teacher will introduce the idea of expressiveness in art. That can be done by asking, "Is it just any house?" Some of the children will say, "No, it's my house"; others may say, "It is the White House." Here the teacher has an opportunity to introduce Rush's (1996) notion that a drawing is an expression of meaning. If it is "my house," then it ought to express "home." If it is the White House, it ought to express "presidency," or something of that sort. Perhaps this is the time to display Grant Wood's *American Gothic*. A principal part of the structure of the making of an art object is its expressiveness.

Social Studies/History. Historians, who interpret the past from the records that remain, are alert to the accuracy and validity of the records they use. Because historians are individuals with convictions, who live in actual cultures, their interpretations differ. When children are asked for the domain within which an historical event is to be considered, they will need enough of the historiographer's concepts, principles, and procedural skills to use the domain well. Suppose that they have selected for study the rise of the labor movement. They will need to consider what records they will consult, the nature of propaganda and counter-propaganda, the state of the economy, the culture of the 1890s, and so on. All of this and more is implied by the specifying question "What field or domain?"

In grade 5, the children are likely to have been studying U.S. history. The comments on historiography above are therefore relevant. But in addition, they might be invited to learn about the culture of the time, including the popular culture—the songs and dance music, the clothing, the place of women, and the like. All of these are included in the concept of the Social Studies, but they are often overlooked.

Literature. The field that the children will enter here is literary criticism, or literary analysis. Since literature is one of the Arts, aesthetic considerations are appropriate: How well do the form, the style, and the content fit one another? The teacher will want to introduce the concepts of form and style, which are likely to be new to the children. One way to introduce these concepts is to ask the children to write in a given style or to outline a form, in this case, of fiction. They might also read the work of excellent critics for their comments on the quality of a given work.

Science. The idea of a domain in Science immediately suggests the "scientific method." There are as many scientific methods as there are scientists, but they all agree that they seek to understand actuality, or reality. The children in this problem-solving discussion are trying to account for the life and death of different plants in the same garden. A class discussion of the problem this presents would be profitable. Should they experiment with plants? Study them closely, under a microscope? Read about the problem? All of these? What plants? What conditions? How much time? The structure of Science involves theorizing, then verifying. These big words belong in the children's vocabulary at this point, for they are about to "make" like scientists.

What Information, or Knowledge, is Required?

Much instruction begins and ends with information, but here it is part of problem solving.

The Arts. This is the part of the problem solving where the children learn what actual artists have done. The middle-grade children doing a drawing of a house have already seen Grant Wood's painting. Perhaps this is the time to bring out the difference between a drawing and a photograph. Although some photographs are expressive (such as the famous Dust Bowl photo of the woman in despair), most are mere uninterpreted records, or snapshots. Given technique, the important quality in art is its expressiveness.

Literature. Literary criticism, which often involves analysis, is the knowledge most available to students. To bring good literature to life, one needs to deepen one's experience of it; able critics share their experience, and how they do it is the relevant knowledge students now require. The problem for students is to develop an informed response to the literature they confront; in this way, their experience will be deepened and will acquire more meaning.

Science. The students are seeking the best answer they can construct to a "Why?" question. The relevant knowledge is always vast in science. In the case imagined here, in which students seek to understand the life and death of plants, the most obvious relevant knowledge is in the life sciences, but there is also a substantial literature derived from the more practical material on gardening. While many gardening books offer only formulas and recipes, the better ones also get into the "why" of it all. Students can learn to make that distinction.

The Social Studies/History. Let us bring together, or integrate, Science and Social Studies, because there is a social side to science. The teacher can ask Social Studies–type questions of our budding scientists. Is there an economy of gardening? There is, if one considers work and time spent as expenditures, and the products of the garden as the rewards. Not all economy involves buying and selling, or exchange of money. That idea is relevant at this point in the students' quest. What about sociology? What is the social nature of garden clubs or of gardeners? Who has gardens and why? The various fields that make up the Social Studies can contribute their knowledge to a deepening of the students' experience.

In the illustration used here, the source of knowledge to be consulted will be the record. Now is the time not only to use the libraries (school and others), but also to dig in the family attic, to consult back copies of newspapers, to ask adults. This is an opportunity to help children get beyond the textbook and use primary sources as much as possible. They might also see how professional historians have treated the problem.

How Shall the Problem Be Restated?

Having considered the goal, the limitations, the field or domain, and the required information, the student is now ready to restate the problem. It is likely that the restated problem will be a plan for action. This plan can be examined by others, and helpful suggestions made. The plan will include the assembly of materials, steps to be taken, an order, a time estimate, and room for changes. Teachers must remember Dewey's warning against slavishly adhering to a plan; let the work, or the solution evolve, but see to it that the direction is appropriate and that the action is not random.

How Shall the Solution to the Problem Be Organized?

The statement of the problem as a plan is also a statement of its organization. At this point, the student looks forward to the completion of the plan and considers how the solution itself shall appear. In the Arts, what shall be done with the completed work? In History, how shall the report be organized? What shall be emphasized, what subordinated? In Literature, as in History, how shall the report of the student's experience be set forth? In what form? How long? What shall be emphasized? In Science, shall the work be organized as an experiment, as a report, or simply as a trial in the garden?

How Will You Know That the Problem Has Been Solved?

This is the climactic question. Ross Mooney once told me that the difference between great and mediocre artists is that the great artists know when to stop. Lesser artists stop too soon, or continue fussing with their work after they should have finished it.

The key term here is evaluation. Students need to learn to evaluate their own work. That's how they grow up. The entire tradition of schooling contradicts this; evaluation is left to the teacher or to some other authority figure. The failure of students to learn to evaluate is at the bottom of the feeling of meaninglessness that afflicts academic work. The literature of problem solving consistently stresses that the more clearly one can see the goal of one's efforts, the more successful the efforts are likely to be. In asking students how they will know that they have solved a problem, we are asking that they evaluate their work, that they state the goal of their efforts clearly enough so that they can recognize it when it is attained.

The importance of this final question cannot be overstated. In the degree that students learn to make their own judgments—their own evaluations—they are behaving like mature people. In the degree that they depend on others to make evaluations for them, they are continuing to act like immature people. It is that simple.

The attempt here has been to consider a central part of the intellectual self and to indicate how some of it can be found within the usual school offering. Every school assignment is a problem to be solved. Problem solving lies at the heart of the tradition of schooling; in the degree that teachers can bring it about among their students, they will have helped them toward mature independence and self-realization.

CHAPTER 8

Toward Depth: A Different Vision

Any practicing teacher, considering the approach described in this book, will object that there simply is not time to do it all. There surely is not, if we continue to try to cover the ground as usual. My answer to this objection is this: *Teach less, and teach it deeper.* Then students may well discover their own humanity. The trouble with the curriculum as it stands is that, in trying to cover too much instead of "uncovering" it, as Earl Kelley often said, the curriculum becomes superficial; it is "merely academic."

This discussion has two main themes; one is technical, the other substantive. Technically, it is proposed here that the terms of the Curriculum Matrix—purpose, substance, and practice—be employed to bring order to a chaotic field. In using the matrix, it is necessary to remember that the curriculum is limitless, boundless, and infinitely interactive, and thus enormously complex. Despite these difficulties, the matrix offers a way of achieving coherence in attempts at curriculum improvement and thereby avoiding the special pleading and incompleteness that has so far afflicted proposed school reforms.

The other theme is substantive. As in any human endeavor, the substance of the Curriculum must be organized around its major purpose, as specified. The major purpose of organized education, it is assumed here, is to bring to reality the full humanity of the individual. To do this, six aspects of the self have been identified, and opportunities to foster growth in each of these have been sought in the usual school subject matter and in other school experience. In the degree that this can be done in school, education will be useful and relevant to life; it will cease being "merely academic." What is called "full humanity" here is often called "maximizing individual potentialities." Students often see the purpose of education as earning high grades or as qualifying for the next step in the educational process. Achieving their full humanity is a more inclusive and a more ambitious goal than these.

Our exploration is inevitably incomplete because of the boundless, complex nature of the field. It is intended only to illustrate how the matrix might be used to achieve the grand purpose of organized education—to bring people to their full humanity. A complete exploration of the field would fill many volumes; it is hoped that the illustrations given here will enable teachers to carry the exploration further, in keeping with their own professional needs.

One of these needs is to bring reality into the classroom. During the twentieth century, teachers have rebelled against the essential narrowness and superficiality of the array of subjects usually taught. They have done two things about these faults: They have tried to integrate the school subjects around practical problems; and they have introduced activities and concerns, chiefly those related to public affairs and citizenship, that go beyond the school subjects as traditionally conceived.

There is no question that the traditional school subjects do not cover everything. As usually offered in school, they are a set of skills and facts and little more, an approach that is basically superficial. These limitations have led many teachers and their students to reject the school subjects as artificial and "merely academic." Although many of the academic skills are necessary for adult living (one must read and write adequately and learn to handle money and make change), the idea that there is more to these school subjects than the school usually offers has been overlooked.

If we will search the usual school subjects for the nature of humanity, or the self, as given in the Curriculum Matrix, the problems of superficiality and artificiality may well be overcome. The school subjects represent disciplined knowledge that goes far beyond the symbol systems, skills, and facts they contain. They are, after all, the best accumulated ways available to penetrate reality. Just acknowledging the actual depth each school subject represents will cause much of the superficiality and artificiality of the offering to vanish. Pursuing the aspects of the self suggested in the matrix offers a way to achieve such depth.

But the school subjects, the disciplines, do not cover everything. Marion Brady (1989, 1993) suggests some practical questions that illustrate this limitation. Considering the topic global warming, he asks his students to confront reality with questions such as whether and in what way moderate global warming might affect a community. Obviously, the more the students can bring to bear on this from experience and study, the better. Much of it will arise from their knowledge of political science, physics, economics, history, literature, and sociology. Each of these disciplines has something to contribute, and the student has to integrate them to make them useful. To such integrated knowledge, the student will add what is available from other experience—what we usually call "common sense." The combination of disciplined knowledge and common sense is what makes educated people useful to themselves and others.

John Raven (1994, chap. 3) identifies a large number of "high-level competencies" required in modern society, none of which is usually identified, or encouraged, in school. All of them are value-based, and all of them are associated with activities that students care about. There are a great many such competencies; they include leadership, communication, reaching agreement, organizing, innovative thinking, peacemaking, and assessing results. It follows that because individuals have different competencies, their potentialities would be brought to reality in a variety of individual enterprises in school.

There is another concern, often expressed, that we must confront: self-esteem. We have noted several times in the foregoing chapters that children and young people are dependent on others for their feelings of personal identity and worth. This will not do. Self-esteem is what results from one's judgments about one's self. The esteem of others is significant, but not enough. The question "Who am I?" haunts children and young people, and some adults, for years on end. In the degree that the answer to that question is in the possession of the one who asks it, self-realization has been achieved; and self-realization is the purpose of education. As we have seen, the self includes the social and moral selves, but it also includes the private selves—the other dimensions of the self. It is the realization of all the dimensions of the self that is sought. That is the realization that constitutes a valid self-esteem.

Practicing teachers, considering these suggestions, may judge that there is not enough time to apply them. Certainly, school time is crowded. Nevertheless, my answer to this problem stands: *Teach less, and teach it deeper.* As we pursue the various dimensions of the self in school subjects, we go deeper and deeper into the subject matter. At the bottom of every subject is the whole self; if we pursue subject matter in depth, subjects will integrate, come alive, and will lose their "merely academic" character. Of course, schooling will continue to include experience not offered in subject matter. But pursued in the depth we suggest here, the academic side of it (which is most of it, after all) will have an importance and a life now largely absent.

The grand purpose of formal education, asserted from the beginning of this book, is the development of a whole self—a self in all its dimensions. From this viewpoint, the school curriculum is a crucial part of the life curriculum, though not the whole. One of the purposes of formal instruction is to lead students into a process of lifelong learning. It is to be hoped that, if the school curriculum has helped students toward self-realization, they will carry their school experience into a successful life curriculum.

References

Alexandrov, D., Kolmogrov, A. H., & Lavrent'ev, H. A. (1962). *Mathematics: Its content, methods, and meaning. Part I: A general view of mathematics analysis* (S. H. Gould, Trans.). Providence, RI: American Mathematical Society.

Almy, M., Chittenden, E., & Miller, P. (1968). *Young children's thinking.* New York: Teachers College Press.

Arnheim, R. (1974). *Art and visual perception.* Berkeley, CA: University of California Press.

Arnstine, D. (1970). Aesthetic qualities and learning. In R. A. Smith (Ed.), *Aesthetic concepts and education* (pp. 21–44). Urbana, IL: University of Illinois Press.

The Association of Teachers of Social Studies in the City of New York (1977). *A handbook for the teaching of social studies* (2nd ed.). Dobkin, W. S., Fischer, J., Ludwig, B., & Kohlinger, R., eds. Boston: Allyn and Bacon.

Barkan, M. (1955). *A foundation for art education.* New York: Ronald Press Company.

Beardsley, M. (1981). *Aesthetics, problems in the philosophy of criticism* (2nd ed.). Indianapolis: Hackett Publishing Company.

Bergamini, D., & the editors of *Life.* (1963). *Mathematics.* New York: Time Inc.

Bloom, B. H. (1981). Peak learning experiences. In *All our children learning* (pp. 195–199). New York: McGraw-Hill.

Bloom, B. H. (Ed.). (1954). *Taxonomy of educational objectives. Handbook I: Cognitive domain.* New York: Longman.

Boorstin, D. (1981). *The discoverers.* New York: Random House.

Boutwell, C. F. (1972). *Getting it all together—the new social studies.* San Rafael, CA: Leswing Press.

Brady, M. (1989). *What's worth teaching?* Albany, NY: State University of New York Press.

Brady, M. (1993). *A study of reality: A supradisciplinary approach.* Kent, WA: Books for Education, Inc.

Bragdon, H. W., & McCutchen, S. P. (1981). *History of a free people.* New York: Macmillan.

Broudy, H. S. (1975). Arts education as artistic perception. In R. L. Leight (Ed.), *Philosophers speak of aesthetic experience in education.* Danville, IL: Interstate Printers.

Brubaker, D. (1963). *Innovation in the social studies: Teachers speak for themselves.* New York: Thomas T. Crowell Company.

81

Buber, M. (1970). *I and thou* (W. Kaufman, Trans.). New York: Scribner.

Buermeyer, L. (1929). *The aesthetic experience* (2nd ed.). Merion, PA: Barnes Foundation.

Corbin, C. R. (1993, November). Clues from dinosaurs, mules, and the bull snake: The field in the twenty-first century. *Quest, 45,* pp. 546–556.

Croce, B. (1983). *Aesthetic as science of expression and general linguistic* (D. Aisnlie, Trans.). Boston: Nonpareil Books. (Original work published 1909)

Davis, P. J., & Hersh, R. (1981). *The mathematical experience.* Boston: Houghton Mifflin.

Davitz, J. B. (1969). *The language of emotion.* New York: The Academic Press.

Deutsch, M. (1973). *The resolution of conflict: Constructive and destructive processes.* New Haven, CT: Yale University Press.

Dewey, J. (1933). *How we think: A restatement of the relation of reflective thinking to the educative process.* Boston: D. C. Heath.

Dewey, J. (1980). *Art as experience.* New York: Perigee. (Original work published 1934)

Eisner, E. W. (1972). *Evaluating artistic vision.* New York, Macmillan.

Eisner, E. W. (Ed.). (1976). *The arts, human development, and education.* Berkeley, CA: McCutchan.

Epstein, J. (1981). *Masters: Portraits of great teachers.* New York: Basic Books.

Eves, H. (1983). *An introduction to the history of mathematics* (5th ed.). New York: CBS College Publishers, Saunders College Publishing.

Fisher, S. (1986). *Development and structure of the body image.* Hillsdale, NJ: Lawrence Erlbaum Associates.

Foshay, A. W. (1978). Intuition and curriculum. In A. W. Foshay & I. Morrissett (Eds.), *Beyond the scientific: A comprehensive view of consciousness.* Boulder, CO: Social Science Education Consortium.

Foshay, A. W. (1991, Summer). The curriculum matrix: Transcendence and mathematics. *Journal of Curriculum and Supervision, 6*(4), 277–295.

Foshay, A. W. (1995, Spring). Aesthetics and history. *Journal of Curriculum and Supervision, 10*(3), 191–206.

Foshay, A. W. (1996, Summer). The physical self and literature. *Journal of Curriculum and Supervision, 11*(4), 341–350.

Foshay, A. W. (1997, Spring). The social self and the human side of science. *Journal of Curriculum and Supervision, 12*(3), 246–255.

Foshay, A. W. (1997, Summer). The emotional self and social studies. *Journal of Curriculum and Supervision, 12*(4), 356–366.

Foshay, A. W. (in press). Problem solving and the arts. *Journal of Curriculum and Supervision.*

Fraley, A. E. (1981). *Schooling and innovation: The rhetoric and the reality.* New York: Tyler Gibson.

Francisco, I. D. (1958). *Art education: Its means and ends.* New York: Harper and Row.

Gallagher, S. (1995). Body schemata and intentionality. In J. L. Bermudez, A. Marcel, & N. Eilen (Eds.), *The body and the self* (pp. 225–244). Cambridge, MA: MIT Press.

Gardner, M. (1982). *Aha! Gotcha! Paradoxes to puzzle and delight*. San Francisco: W. H. Freeman.

Glick, J. (1987). *Chaos: Making a new science*. New York: Penguin.

Gogol, N. V. (1925). The cloak. In Thomas Seltzer (Ed.), *Best russian short stories* (pp. 40–81). New York: Modern Library.

Graff, H. J. (1967). *The free and the brave*. Chicago: Rand McNally.

Guillen, M. (1983). *Bridges to infinity, the human side of mathematics*. Boston: Houghton Mifflin.

Hagstrom, W. O. (1965). *The scientific community*. Edwardsville, IL: Southern Illinois University Press.

Hale, S. (1839). *History of the United States from their first settlement as colonies to the close of the war with Great Britain in 1815*. Keene, NH: J. & J. W. Prentiss.

Hofstadter, D. R. (1979). *Gödel, Escher, Bach: An eternal golden braid*. New York: Random House.

Hofstadter, D. R., Miller, W., & Aaron, D. (1970). *The American republic* (Vol. 1) (2nd ed.). Englewood Cliffs, NJ: Prentice-Hall.

Izard, C. E. (1991). *The psychology of emotions*. New York: Plenum.

Jacobs, H. L. (1970). *Mathematics: A human endeavor*. San Francisco: W. H. Freeman.

Jenness, D. (1990). *Making sense of social studies*. New York: Macmillan.

Jersild, A. T. (1952). *In search of self*. New York: Bureau of Publications, Teachers College, Columbia University.

Jersild, A. T., & Holmes, F. S. (1935). Children's fears. *Child Development Monographs*, 20.

Johnson, M. (1987). *The body in the mind*. Chicago, IL: The University of Chicago Press.

Johnson, S. (1766). *Dictionary of the English Language (Vol. II)*. London: A. Miller and others.

Jonassen, D. H. (1997). Instructional design models for well-structured and ill-structured problem-solving learning outcomes. *Educational Technology: Research and Development*, *45*, 65–94,

Jones, P. D. (1973). *Rediscovering ritual*. New York: Newman Press.

Kagan, J. (1984). *The nature of the child*. New York: Basic Books.

Kahney, H. (1993). *Problem solving: Current issues* (2nd ed.). Buckingham, UK: Open University Press.

Kaufman, F. (1978). *The infinite in mathematics and its elimination*. Dordrecht, Netherlands: D. Reidel.

Kay, A. W. (1969). *Moral development*. New York: Schocken.

Keyser, C. J. (1925). *The human worth of rigorous thinking* (2nd ed.). New York: Columbia University Press.

Klein, M. (1978). *Mathematics: An introduction to its spirit and use*. San Francisco: W. H. Freeman.

Kohlberg, L. (1981). *Essays on moral development: Vol. 1. The philosophy of moral development: Moral stages and the idea of justice*. San Francisco: Harper and Row.

Kohlberg, L. (1984). *Essays on moral development: Vol. 2. The psychology of moral development: The nature and validity of moral stages*. San Francisco: Harper and Row.

Krout, J. A. (1935). *An outline history of the United States to 1865* (Rev. ed.). New York: Barnes and Noble.

Kuhn. T. (1970). *International encyclopedia of unified science: Foundations of the unity of science: Vol. 2, no. 2. The structure of scientific revolutions* (2nd ed.).Chicago: University of Chicago Press.

Langer, S. (1957). *Problems of art*. London: Kegan Paul.

Langfeld, H. S. (1967). *The aesthetic attitude*. Washington, NY: Kennikut Press. (Original work published 1920)

Lawton, D., & Dufour, H. (1976). *The new social studies* (2nd ed.). London: Heinemann.

Lowenfeld, V. (1947). *Creative and mental growth*. New York: Macmillan.

Maslow, A. H. (1968). *Toward a psychology of being*. New York: Van Nostrand.

Maslow, A. H. (1971). *The farther reaches of human nature*. New York: Penguin.

May, E. R. (1989). *A proud nation* [teacher's edition]. Evanston, IL: McDougal, Little.

Methany, E. (1968). *Movement and meaning*. New York: McGraw-Hill.

Miles, J. (1965). *Wordsworth and the vocabulary of emotion*. University of California Publications in English. (Original work published 1942)

Miles, J. (1983). *Collected poems, 1930–1983*. Bloomington, IN: Indiana University Press.

Munro, T. (1956). *Art education, its philosophy and psychology*. New York: Liberal Arts Press.

Nagel, E. (1968). *The structure of science*. New York: Harcourt, Brace and World.

Nagel, E., & Newman, J. R. (1959). *Gödel's proof*. New York: New York University Press.

Noddings, N. (1992). *Challenge to the caring school*. New York: Teachers College Press.

Noddings, N. (1995, May). Teaching themes of care. *Kappan 76*(9), 675–679.

Noddings, N., & Shore, P. J. (1984). *Awakening the inner eye in education*. New York: Teachers College Press.

Otto, R. (1923). *The idea of the holy*. London: Oxford University Press.

Phenix, P. (1964). *Realms of meaning*. New York: McGraw-Hill.

Phenix, P. (1974). Transcendence and the curriculum. In E. W. Eisner and E. Vallance (Eds.), *Conflicting conceptions of curriculum* (pp. 00–00). Berkeley: McCutchan.

Piaget, J. (1954). *The construction of reality in the child*. New York: Basic Books.

Piaget, J. (1965). *The moral development of the child* (M. Gibson, Trans.). New York: Free Press.

Plato. (1935). *The republic, Book VII*. (A. D. Lindsay, Trans.) [Everyman Edition]. London: J. H. Dent.

Pole, D. (1975). The concept of reason. In R. F. Deardon, P. H. Hirst, & R. S. Peters (Eds.), *Reason* (pp. 1–25). London and Boston: Routledge and Kegan Paul.

Popp, W. (1975). *The history of mathematics: Topics for schools* (M. Bruckheimer, Trans.). London: Transworld.

Raven, J. (1994). *Managing education for effective schooling*. Oxford: Oxford Psychologists Press.

Rush, J. C. (1996). Conceptual consistency and problem solving: Tools to evaluate learning in studio art. In D. Bougthon, E. W. Eisner, & J. Ligtvoet (Eds.), *Evaluating and assessing the visual arts in education* (pp. 42–53). New York: Teachers College Press.

Samuel, W. (1981). *Personality: Searching for the source of human behavior*. New York: McGraw-Hill.

Smith, H. (1977). *Forgotten truth*. New York: Harper.

Smith, H. (1982). *Beyond the post-modern mind*. New York: Crossroad.

Smith, R. A. (Ed.). (1970). *Aesthetic concepts and education*. Urbana, IL: University of Illinois Press.

Stein, S. K. (1969). *Mathematics: The man-made universe* (2nd ed.). San Francisco: W. H. Freeman.

Swinton, W. (1880). *A condensed school history of the United States*. New York: Ivison, Blakeman, Taylor & Co.

Tillich, P. (1959). *Theology of culture*. London: Oxford University Press.

Thornton, S. J. (1994). The social studies near century's end. In L. Darling-Hammond (Ed.), *Review of research in education, 20* (pp. 223–254). Washington, DC: American Educational Research Association.

Toynbee, A. J. (1960). *A study of history* (Abridgment by D. C. Somervell). London: Oxford University Press.

Underhill, E. (1982). *Worship*. New York: Crossroad.

Watson, J. D. (1968). *The double helix: A personal account of the discovery of the structure of DNA*. New York: Atheneum.

West, M. (1982). Meditation and self-awareness. In Underwood, G. (Ed.), *Aspects of consciousness* (Vol.5, pp. 199–232). London: Academic Press.

Whitman, W. (1959). *Leaves of grass* (M. Cowley, Ed.). New York: Viking. (Originally published in 1855)

Woods, D. R. (1987). How might I teach problem solving? In J. Stiles (Ed.), *Developing critical thinking and problem-solving abilities* (p. 55). San Francisco: Jossey-Bass

Wordsworth, W. (1907). The complete poetical works of William Wordsworth. London: Macmillan and Co.

Wright, R. (1966). *Native son*. New York: Harper.

Zevin, J. (1992). *Social studies for the twenty-first century*. New York: Longman.

Index

About the Author

The education career of Arthur Wellesley Foshay spanned 62 years, ending with his death in 1998 at age 85. He rose through the professional ranks as teacher, guidance counselor, principal, professor, and dean. During his tenure at the Ohio State University and Teachers College, Columbia University, he served as consultant to the U.S. Office of Education and to the Ford Foundation in Iran, as well as to several school districts and two local school boards. He was successively president of the Association for Supervision and Curriculum Development and the John Dewey Society, and he maintained an ongoing active membership in the American Educational Association (AERA). He was co-founder of the International Association for the Evaluation of Educational Attainment (IEA) and directed its pilot study. His published works include more than a hundred journal articles, four books, and contributions to many other books.